Culture and politics in Northern Ireland

1960–1990

Ideas and Production

Over recent years the study of the humanities has changed beyond all recognition for many of us. The increasing attention given to theories of interpretation and writing has altered the intellectual circumstances and perspectives of the various disciplines which compose the group. The studies of literature, history, society, politics, gender and philsophy are increasingly finding common ground in shared assumptions about intellectual procedure and method. **Ideas and Production** addresses this common ground.

We are interested in the investigation of the particular historical circumstances which produce the culture of a period or group, and the exploration of conventionally unregarded or understudied work. We are also interested in the relationship of intellectual movements to institutions, and the technological and economic means of their production. It is through the study of the circumstances and conditions in which ideas are realised that the humanities can develop fresh approaches in a period of rapid and exciting social and intellectual change.

As thought and learning become increasingly international and older political and intellectual structures give way, **Ideas and Production** is concerned to investigate new intellectual horizons from the perspective of competing theories and methods, and through the rethinking of old or settled definitions.

Ideas and Production welcomes the potential of debate and intervention, as well as the careful study of materials. The series is aimed at the student, teacher and general reader and encourages clarity and directness in argument, language and method.

Edward J. Esche, Penelope Kenrick, Rick Rylance,
Nigel Wheale

Culture and politics in Northern Ireland
1960–1990

Edited by Eamonn Hughes

Open University Press
Milton Keynes · Philadelphia

Ideas and Production is published by
Open University Press in collaboration with
Anglia Higher Education College

Open University Press
Celtic Court
22 Ballmoor
Buckingham
MK18 1XW

941. 60824
C968

and
1900 Frost Road, Suite 101
Bristol, PA 19007, USA

First published 1991

British Library Cataloguing in Publication Data

Culture and politics in Northern Ireland, 1960–1990.–
    (Ideas and productions).
    1. Northern Ireland, history
    I. Hughes, Eamonn.   II. Series
    941.6

    ISBN 0–335–09712–X

Library of Congress Cataloging-in-Publication Data

Culture and politics in Northern Ireland, 1960–1990/edited by Eamonn
    Hughes.
        p.   cm. – (Ideas and production)
    Includes index.
    ISBN 0–335–09712–X (pb)
    1. Northern Ireland – Politics and government – 1969–.
    2. Northern Ireland – Civilization.
    I. Hughes, Eamonn, 1955–.   II. Series.
    DA990.U46C85   1991
    941.60824 – dc   90–21661   CIP

Typeset by Scarborough Typesetting Services
Printed in Great Britain by St Edmundsbury Press,
Bury St Edmunds, Suffolk

Contents

Contributors

Professor George Boyce was Head of the Department of Political Theory and Government at University College, Swansea, 1982–5 and 1988–9. He is the author of a number of works on the history and politics of Ireland. He is also a member of the Executive Committee of the British Association for Irish Studies.

Joseph Ruane is a lecturer in the Department of Social Theory and Institutions at University College Cork.

Jennifer Todd is a lecturer in the Department of Politics in University College Dublin.

James White McAuley is a lecturer in Sociology at St Mary's College, Strawberry Hill and is a member of the Executive Committee of the British Association for Irish Studies.

Jonathan Moore is a freelance lecturer, writer and broadcaster on Irish affairs. He is editor of the journal *Irish Studies in Britain* and a British editor of the *Irish Literary Supplement*. His edited book *All Ireland* was published in 1988 and he is currently writing a book on the politics of extradition.

Monica McWilliams lectures in the Department of Social Administration and Policy at the University of Ulster at Jordanstown and has been actively involved with women's groups throughout Northern Ireland.

Hazel Morrissey is a Research Officer with the Transport and General Workers Union in Belfast. Following her primary degree she spent four years as a research student at Queen's University,

Belfast and has recently completed an M.Sc in Labour Market Studies at the University of Ulster.

Seán Hutton is a writer and Irish language poet who is currently Executive Director of the British Association for Irish Studies.

Shaun Richards lectures in the Department of Humanities at Staffordshire Polytechnic. He is co-author of *Writing Ireland*. He is a member of the Executive Committee of the British Association for Irish Studies.

Liam O'Dowd is a lecturer in the Department of Social Studies at the Queen's University of Belfast.

Cover illustration by Simon Grayley, cover design by Will Hill.

Text illustrations

Jonathan Harris	14
Wendy Howarth	26
Ben Clowes	44
Joanne Karran	70
Juliet Simmons	82
Paul Pickersgill	102
David Williams	120
Joanne Karran	138
Paul Pickersgill	152

Art Editor: Will Hill

Acknowledgements

The editors acknowledge the help of the following individuals and organisations who have assisted in the production of *Culture and Politics in Northern Ireland*: the Arts Council of Northern Ireland for a generous grant towards production costs; Mike Salmon, Tom Allcock, Steve Marshall of Anglia Higher Education College, Cambridge, and Ray Cunningham and Sue Hadden of the Open University Press, for their material support in establishing Ideas and Production as a Series; Ian Gordon, Head of the Department of English, Communication and Performing Arts, AHEC, for his consistent support for the project; the Computer Centre, School of Art and Design, and Division of Graphic Reproduction and Printing, AHEC, for invaluable help in the production process, particularly Clive Bray, Richard Boase, Mike Button, John Elstone, Andy Geliher, Ian Kitching, Nicky Morland, Gordon Shaw, and Colin Wood and the BTEC HND Illustration students and course administrators.

The editor and publishers are grateful to the following for permission to quote copyright material:

Blackstaff Press for extracts from:
John Boyd, *Out of My Class* (Belfast, 1985)
The Selected John Hewitt (ed. Alan Warner) (Belfast, 1981)
John Hewitt, *Freehold and Other Poems* (Belfast, 1986)
Dolmen for extracts from:
John Montague, *The Rough Field*, 3rd edn (Dublin, 1979)
Faber and Faber for extracts from:
Robert Harbinson, *No Surrender* (London, 1960)
Seamus Heaney, *North* (London, 1975)

Seamus Heaney, *Selected Poems, 1965–1975* (London, 1980)
Seamus Heaney, *The Haw Lantern* (London, 1987)
Tom Paulin, *The Strange Museum* (London, 1980)
Tom Paulin, *Liberty Tree* (London, 1983)
Field Day for extracts from:
Ireland's Field Day (London, Hutchinson, 1985)
Terry Eagleton, *Saint Oscar* (Derry, 1989)
Foilseachain Náisiúnta Teoranta for extracts from:
Breandán O Doiblin, *Néal Maidine agus Tine Oíche* (Dublin, 1964)
Gallery Press for extracts from:
Ciaran Carson, *Belfast Confetti* (Oldcastle, Co. Meath, 1989)
Salamander Press for extracts from:
Michael Longley, *Poems 1963–1983* (Harmondsworth,
Penguin, 1986)

Every reasonable effort has been made to obtain permission for
copyright material when the amount quoted may be in excess of
'fair dealing'. The editor and publishers apologise to copyright
holders for any oversight.

1

Introduction: Northern Ireland – border country

Eamonn Hughes

In the late 1960s it seemed as if Northern Ireland was merely the seat of what Seamus Heaney called 'anachronistic passions'.[1] The most prevalent perception of Northern Ireland was that it was a tightly-enclosed province bounded by outworn loyalties and obscure allegiances. The passions underpinning those loyalties and allegiances were fierce, impenetrable and embarrassing in equal measures. Even in the South of Ireland, the most common perception of the North was that it belonged to a category of one.[2] In Glenn Patterson's novel *Burning Your Own* this image is expressed through the central figure, the 10-year old Mal Martin, watching the Apollo moon landing at about the time that others were watching the British Army marching onto a territory seemingly even more distinct from, and alien to, the 'modern world'.[3]

This image of Northern Ireland as a recalcitrantly regressive place somehow separate from the modern progressive world, has always been partially balanced by a weaker, and more often internally-generated, sense of it as a place in which the border being disputed is precisely that between modernising forces and ancient passions. In this view the Civil Rights marches were associated with the Black American civil-rights marches, were of a piece with 'les événements' of 1968, the Grosvenor Square riots and so on.[4] This weaker image has been challenged on the grounds that hindsight, and our knowledge of the developments arising from the late 1960s, shows that a somewhat different agenda was being constructed in Northern Ireland. However, a consideration of the North in the 1960s and since must acknowledge that there was an awareness of broader social, cultural and political issues than simply those operating within Northern Ireland.

A personal memory which crystallises for me this latter sense of Northern Ireland as a place straddling the anachronistic and the contemporary may serve as an illustration of what I mean. The local cinema on the Woodstock Road in East Belfast, a staunchly, and, in the early 1970s, violently loyalist area, shared premises with the Headquarters of the local Unionist Party. Both the cinema, The Woodstock, and the Unionist Party HQ were housed in a forbidding black-basalt fronted building, which evinced the monolithic style of the Unionist Party. The existence of the cinema always seemed an affront to this style, but never more so than when its display case, like thousands all over the world at the time, contained a poster proclaiming 'Woodstock – 3 Days of Love, Peace and Music'. This phrase still serves to sum up a generation, and it has to be remembered that members of that generation lived in Northern Ireland and could be struck by this ironical conjunction. The Woodstock ethos, if it ever existed, has long since dissipated. If the first image of Northern Ireland as separate and anachronistic that I outlined above was correct then I should be able to point to the way in which the truly indigenous Northern Irish elements in this memory outlasted the fragile hippy ethos; the point of the memory would be that the exotic import from the modern world could not survive the fierce blasts of the local climate. This is not the case. The building which housed the Unionist Party and the cinema has gone, a victim of the fragmentation and consequent economic weakening of the Unionist Party, of the decline in cinema-going throughout the developed world, and of the widespread urban redevelopment of the past twenty years. The single story shop units which now occupy the site are a commonplace of banal urban planning. Every element in the memory has altered or disappeared and the one thing that remains is the still-relevant memory of the juxtaposition of the indigenous and the international. The contradictions revealed in this memory remain in other forms and are ranged on either side of the numerous borders which run through Northern Ireland, of which the one between it and the Republic of Ireland is in many ways the least important. This 'line on the grass', in Tom Paulin's phrase,[5] is certainly no more substantial than any of the others.

The subject of the present volume is, among other things, some of the many borders which criss-cross Northern Ireland, and the ways in which they, like all borders, have shifted, crumbled, and yet continue both to divide and to bring about curious juxtapositions. If the Northern Ireland of the late 1960s can be, however glibly, paralleled by wider international movements, it seems that the same can be said for the Northern Ireland of the early 1990s. This is a time when we have been forced to recognise that borders are fragile phenomena, but that people's need for them remains strong. Borders as phenomena called into being by affective needs are often the boundaries of ghettoes; borders recognised as arbitrary are a condition of what we have come to call the postmodern world. Northern Ireland exists as both a ghetto and as a postmodern entity. Far from being a region sealed in a timewarp, it increasingly appears that Northern Ireland, in the Europe (both West and increasingly East) of the nations, may well be a message for the future.

The Northern Ireland that is considered in this volume is therefore not only the ghetto bordered by the line on the grass. It is also a modern place with the pluralities, discontents, and linkages appropriate to a modern place. The borders which it straddles, of language, of gender, of party politics, of social structures, are the boundaries which run through any modern society, although they twist and turn in ways particular to Northern Ireland. Northern Ireland as a whole is not so much enclosed by its borders as defined by them: it is a border country.

The divisions commonly held to be peculiar to Northern Ireland – Protestant/Catholic, Nationalist/Unionist, Republican/Loyalist, Irish/British – are also linkages peculiar to it. Richard Kearney in his introduction to *The Irish Mind* states that it is a characteristic of the Irish to see any choice as always containing three terms: either, or, and both. The choice most commonly made by the Irish is neither either nor or but both.[6] Northern Ireland we may say is neither either nor or; its full definition is both. As Seamus Deane has said, it is 'Ulster's peculiar fate – to be neither Irish nor British while also being both.'[7] In consequence, Northern Ireland is a place in which identity does not confront difference; rather identity is difference. In a recent work on the theory of the relations between modes of narration and national identity, Homi K. Bhabha commented that 'The "other" is never outside or beyond us; it emerges forcefully, within cultural discourse, when we *think* we speak most intimately and indigenously "between ourselves".'[8] This speaks directly to the situation within Northern Ireland, where identity must always be formed on terms of intimacy with whatever one chooses to regard as the other. Far from making Northern Ireland a peculiar place, from which the modern world turns embarrassed equally by its anachronism and passion, this makes it central to the experience of the modern world.

> But we who are modern live increasingly in a discontinuous, polyglot world, and what is now clear to me is that the experience . . . of confused loyalties and uncertain identity, is not, as I once thought, aberrant. In a world often politically and culturally disrupted it is an experience which becomes increasingly typical.[9]

This plural and dynamic identity can be traced through manifestations in various domains: linguistic, historical, social, and, the primary concern of this introduction, cultural. Confusion, one of Brian Friel's characters says, is not an ignoble condition, especially if it is welcomed as an alternative to the disablement brought about by attempting to live in a secure but inaccurately-mapped landscape.[10] Faced with the richness of Northern Ireland one cannot hope to produce an accurate map, but one can do more than merely reproduce 'Baedekers of the nightmare ground'.[11]

The cultural address that has been made to Northern Ireland is not a simple one. If one wishes to see traces of a forward- and outward-looking consciousness in Northern Ireland, one has also to acknowledge the introspective and backward elements of that same consciousness. This is not to say that one is balancing the good against the bad, for in matters of identity the bases of value judgements are notoriously unstable. There are elements of the culture which are introspective and backward-looking without necessarily being malign; indeed they are positively healthy. However, it is not the purpose of this introduction (nor, indeed, of the volume) to be comprehensive. Rather, this introduction aims, like the volume, to interrogate the idea of Northern Ireland as a place apart. I wish therefore to consider some recent trends within Northern Irish writing which turn away from the introspective and backward-looking nature of much that has gone before.

It is necessary to begin with some sense of what these recent trends react against. W. J. McCormack has referred to the idea of 'Ulster as autonomous text' and has stated that 'Not many have considered the possibility that the violence in Irish society . . . is part of a broader pattern in Western society. The result has been that the debate on Irish affairs is conducted in a remarkably inward fashion.'[12] This has resulted in literary representations of Northern Ireland as an enclosed and, more importantly, static and therefore somehow complete region. The most famous of such representations are the 'archeological' poems of Seamus Heaney in which the answers which the poet seeks are to be found by delving ever deeper into the ground of Northern Ireland. This can lead to a form of cherished self-pity as the principal response to events in the North:

> Is there a life before death? That's chalked up
> In Ballymurphy. Competence with pain,
> Coherent miseries, a bite and sup,
> We hug our little destiny again.[13]

Nor was Heaney alone in this form of representation. His archaeological enquiries rely on an implicit essentialism which has its counterparts in Derek Mahon's anthropological concerns[14] and in John Hewitt's examination of the 'exact geology' of the 'faulted ledge' that is Northern Ireland.[15]

In each of these sets of images there is a strong sense that the endeavour of the writer is a form of field work (the title of one of Heaney's collections) which will yield only what is already buried or sown. This in turn chimes with the centrality of the field in Northern Irish culture. Orange marches are always to 'the field' (in reality, numerous fields scattered across Northern Ireland) where speeches are made, prayers said, and memories of the field of battle renewed. Nationalists on the other hand mourn the separation of the fourth green field (the ancient province of Ulster) from the other three fields of Ireland (the provinces of Leinster, Munster and Connaught). The image of the field combines the agricultural concerns of the Northern Irish with the sense of the North as a place of battle: 'two men fighting over a field'.[16] No museum of Northern Ireland can be complete without both senses. So in John Hewitt's 'Cultra Manor: the Ulster Folk Museum' is replete with agricultural implements, 'What they need now, somewhere about here, / is a field for the faction fights.'[17] The overall sense generated by this prevalent image of the field is that Northern Ireland is a site of division but is static because it has achieved its fate.

Northern Ireland is reduced to a site on which, while arguments about ownership are carried on, field workers accumulate fragments and shards of a past which is capable only of reinforcing the present. This goes some way, I think, to explaining one of the gaps in the literary culture of the North. While poetry and drama have once again produced responses to turmoil in Ireland, the novel seems, once again, to have shied away from the matter of (Northern) Ireland. The major response to Northern Ireland on the part of novelists has been in the form of the thriller. This is a genre in which there is a minimum requirement for a plausible locale for 'agents in the field'. To put this another way, what is needed is no more than an adventure playground in which 'heroes' can confront 'villains'. At its most mechanical the thriller moves to a closure which projects its locale as a closed but always unresolved system: the Cold War can never end, the forces of corruption can never be defeated, and the problems of Northern Ireland will inevitably endure. To take one example of this mechanical form of thriller, Tom Clancy's *Patriot Games*,[18] uses events in the North to drive its plot, but not one scene is set in Northern Ireland. The plot concerns the plan by a Maoist off-shoot of the Provisional IRA to assassinate Prince Charles, and to wipe out the leadership of the Provisionals. The climax involves Prince Charles and others in a high-speed boat chase after his would-be assassins. But, in a novel which is longer than Roy Foster's *Modern Ireland*, Clancy seems unable to find time to inform us of the outcome of the secondary plot in Northern Ireland. The contempt displayed is obvious and uninteresting, but what is important is the projection of Northern Ireland as a fated place of always-unfinished business, static and unresolved. This risible novel would not concern us if it were not for the fact that so many of the novels produced in Northern Ireland rely on the form or mechanics of the thriller, for reasons which are very similar to those underpinning Clancy's novel.

Three examples by now-established novelists will serve to illustrate this point. In Benedict Kiely's *Proxopera*[19] a family is held hostage while the grandfather is sent to plant a proxy bomb. In Bernard MacLaverty's *Cal*[20] the central figure is an unwilling but still culpable accomplice in the murder of a police reservist whose affair with his victim's widow is also a flirtation with discovery. Most recently, Brian Moore's *Lies of Silence*[21] once again involves hostage-taking and a proxy bombing as a moment of crisis. Each of these novels connects with the contemporary details of Northern Ireland largely through its reliance on the conventions of the thriller, and in each case a separate novel is overlaid by those conventions. *Proxopera* is a lament for a non-existent *haute-bourgeois* past of sun-drenched lawns and lakes; it is in fact a Big House novel with a contemporary twist. *Cal* is a study of the complexities and guilts of first love with the added savour of murder. *Lies of Silence* is a novel about divorce – a variant on Graham Greene's *The Heart of the Matter* – in which violence again increases the pressure of emotional circumstances but does not alter them. In each case, to a greater or lesser degree, 'ordinary' lives are intruded upon by violence, but do not interact dynamically with the circumstantial reality of that violence. It is as if having taken over the idea of Northern Ireland as static and complete but unresolved, the novelists have left themselves little room to insinuate their characters into the specifics of the North, and have to resort to the conventions of the thriller to establish a footing on the treacherous surface which they have accepted. The failing of the novel in regard to Northern Ireland is that, by accepting the image of the North as fated, it has not allowed for the interplay of characters, form and circumstances.

None of this is to deny that the thriller can often articulate a rich response to a morally and politically complex world. But significantly it is a poet, Paul Muldoon, who has best mobilised the thriller's conventions. For his apparent dandyism, with its penchant for genre-napping, is often underpinned by the moral seriousness of the thrillers which he parodically appropriates to his hallucinatory narrative poems.[22] The significance of this has to do with the way in which the novelists have been more accepting of the idea of Northern Ireland as enclosed.

Three recent first novels can, however, be set against the previous trio to suggest a way out of the impasse of a closed form failing to gain a purchase on an apparently static but unresolved society. Glenn Patterson's *Burning Your Own*, Robert McLiam Wilson's *Ripley Bogle*,[23] and Danny Morrison's *West Belfast*[24] are as oddly assorted as the first trio but share a number of interesting elements. In each case there is an emphasis on the child's perspective on the North; in the first two cases the action is contained within the space of days; in the last two cases the diary or journal is an important formal element; and in all three cases the novelists allow their characters to witness the origins of the present violence, and to set those origins against a society which is marked by divisions of class as well as sectarianism.

While Kiely, MacLaverty and Moore attempt to respond to the fact of violence, Patterson, McLiam Wilson and Morrison respond to its circumstances. The former novelists begin *in media res,* giving the impression of Northern Ireland as being in the grip of a never-begun, never-ending fate; the latter novelists deal with violence as a recurrent but not fated part of the circumstances of existence in the North. The former take as their subjects adults who are already freighted with their own problems and concerns and add the problem of violence, thereby producing an earnestly responsible but utterly conventional moral response. The latter, by adopting a child's perspective for at least part of their narratives, enable themselves to abdicate from moralising. The difference in terms of both form and language, is that Patterson, McLiam Wilson and Morrison avoid that language of exhausted fatalism identified by Seamus Deane as one of the principal obstacles to dynamic debate in Northern Ireland.[25]

Kiely, MacLaverty and Moore's novels rely on a conventonal form and a set of conventional autonomies: Northern Ireland, the text, the individual, each of which is placed under threat by the presence of violence, which must therefore be simply resisted. Patterson, McLiam Wilson and Morrison eschew these conventional autonomies. Their texts escape the sense of Northern Ireland as fatalistically complete by taking for granted that the world beyond the North – the world of moon landings, the Beatles, London in the 1960s and 1980s – is a part of the Northern Irish experience. Each text also refuses the conventional closure offered by the thriller plot, as the novelists play with form and language, allowing each to be deformed by what it has to carry. Finally, their characters rather than being simply threatened by violence are equally formed by it, finding it to be one more aspect of a process of development. These three works therefore go beyond the surface morality of the works by Kiely, MacLaverty and Moore to a more profound moral and political response to an encompassing but often resisted framework of determinations linking the inner and outer lives of their characters.

All of this is to say that novelists appear to be learning some of the lessons already mastered by the playwrights and poets. Each of the novelists evinces an interest in geography, a necessary science once one begins to move beyond the enclosed domain of the field. Ripley Bogle's tramps around London are one form of this concern. The children in *West Belfast* and Mal Martin both climb the hills around Belfast and see it as a web of connections. In this they share an emerging concern with mapping evident in the work of a number of poets and play-wrights as they too move beyond field work.

In this regard the best place to turn is to a work which at first appears to be another instance of field work. John Montague's *The Rough Field* is rough not only with regard to the texture of the history uncovered in it, it is equally rough in outline. Its boundaries are extensive and subject to change: 'lines of protest / lines of change / . . . Berkeley . . . Berlin / Paris, Chicago / seismic waves / zigzagging through / a faulty world'.[26] Montague's 'faulty world' answers to and extends Hewitt's fatalistic 'faulted ledge'. But Hewitt himself came to see that 'the whole tarnished map is stained and torn, / never to be read as pastoral again'.[27] This, alongside Montague's catalogue of place names, also marks a shift from the rural to the urban which goes with the concern with mapping. Friel's *Translations* is famously concerned with the Ordnance Survey of Ireland in 1833, but he is not the only playwright to be so concerned. Henry Joy McCracken in Stewart Parker's *Northern Star* immediately before his execution imagines a walk through Belfast which reveals his love for the place despite his sense that it is 'Brain-damaged and dangerous, continuously violating itself, a place of perpetual breakdown.'[28] This intro-duces another element which is important in this trend towards images of mapping, the recognition that maps enable one to move beyond borders and to break free from fatalism into a realm of fluidity and change.

In *Belfast Confetti* Ciaran Carson concentrates on Belfast but not as a stable, originary place. He describes it as being built on 'sleech' and with these foundations it can never be anything but 'a revised version of itself' for 'to-day's plan is already yester-day's'. In these circumstances it is impossible ever to map accurately anything so mutable as a city, so the city becomes the only map of the city.[29]

This new welcoming of fluidity and change allows the North-ern writer to confront what is, rather than what ought to be. This literary shift, from a sense of the North as fated to a complete but unresolved identity, to a sense of it as being at the intersection of borders, is evident in much recent poetry. The most recent volumes by Heaney, Paulin and Muldoon are all concerned with the crossing of cultural and political borders, and a sense of identity as being always founded on difference, a difference which Heaney for one has now internalised: 'is it any wonder when I thought / I would have second thoughts?'[30] This is no longer a statement of reticence, shyness or indecision in the face of the 'other', but a richly ambiguous statement of the always-at-least-dual nature of the Northern Irish and their cultures, which is made possible by the recognition that borders can be crossed.

The essays

Contributors to this volume were asked to consider, from within their own area of expertise, the question of Northern Ireland as a place apart. Their essays taken together demonstrate the multifarious nature of the borders running through Northern Ireland and show the ways in which many of those borders have been deliberately constructed in an attempt to prevent the realities of Northern Ireland challenging received wisdom both about it and about the ways in which it intersects with the wider world. **George Boyce** sets out the case for a new conceptual framework for a history of Northern Ireland which would lead to a recasting of the history of Ireland, Britain and beyond. **Joe Ruane and Jennifer Todd** argue that cultural analyses of Northern Ireland both obscure the true situation in the North and suggest that other societies are naturally more 'tolerant'. Their countervailing argument for a structural analysis shifts responsibility onto those who hold power rather than those who are affected by it. From these articles on conceptual frameworks we move to two papers on political reponses to the situation in the North. **Jim McAuley's** examination of the cultural origins of the UDA and its implication in the political debates within the protestant working class reveals it as an organisation which is subject to the structural forces within Northern Irish politics. **Jon Moore's** overview of the British Labour Party's response to Northern Ireland shows how the mainstream of the Party wished to keep a *cordon sanitaire* between itself and the North. This self-protective indifference has helped to sustain conservative social attitudes and legislation within the North. The next two essays deal with the ways in which women in Northern Ireland have been affected by this. **Monica McWilliams** describes the social, legislative and religious determinants which have shaped not only the lives of individual women, but also the development of the women's movement. She concludes that the exclusion of women from politics cannot continue. **Hazel Morrissey**, focusing on the economic situation of women, foresees the collapse of borders as the main hope for women in this regard. The final three essays of the volume consider aspects of the cultural domain. **Seán Hutton's** survey of the novel in Irish shows how it has developed to the point at which it can deal with the topic of Northern Ireland, something which, it can be argued, the novel in English has only just begun to do. **Shaun Richards** considers the idea of the fifth province which underwrites the work of the Field Day company, but he challenges the idea that this can foster a radical pluralism. Finally, **Liam O'Dowd** writes about the role of intellectuals in promoting a plurality of cultures in Northern Ireland and the ways in which this has served to reduce their political impact. This stringent criticism is a perhaps despairing but almost certainly realistic final word for such a volume.

Acknowledgements

Formal acknowledgement to the publishers and authors who have given permission for their work to be quoted is made elsewhere. Here I should like to thank those who made this volume possible. First and foremost I wish to thank the contributors who responded with generosity and creativity to the initial idea of a volume on Northern Ireland. I also wish to thank the editorial board of *Ideas and Production*, Ed Esche, Rick Rylance, and Nigel Wheale, who took up the idea for the volume with alacrity and then worked with equal patience to bring it to publication.

References

1. Seamus Heaney, 'Delirium of the Brave', *The Listener*, 27 November 1969, 757–759.
2. Clare O'Halloran, *Partition and the Limits of Irish Nationalism: An Ideology under Stress* (Dublin, Gill and Macmillan, 1987), ch. 1.
3. Glenn Patterson, *Burning Your Own* (London, Chatto and Windus, 1988), p. 203.
4. Gerry Adams, *The Politics of Irish Freedom* (Dingle, Brandon, 1986), pp. 9–10.
5. Tom Paulin, 'Line on the Grass', *The Strange Museum* (London, Faber and Faber, 1980), p. 20.
6. Richard Kearney, ed., *The Irish Mind: Exploring Intellectual Traditions* (Dublin, Wolfhound, 1985), p. 9.
7. Seamus Deane, 'The Artist and the Troubles', in Tim Pat Coogan, ed., *Ireland and the Arts: A Literary Review Special Issue* (London, Namara Press, n.d.), pp. 45–6.

8. Homi K. Bhabha, 'Introduction: narrating the nation', in Homi K. Bhabha, ed., *Nation and Narration* (London, Routledge, 1990), p. 4.

9. George J. Watson, 'Cultural Imperialism: An Irish View', *The Yale Review*, (1986), 516.

10. Brian Friel, *Translations*, in his *Selected Plays* (London, Faber and Faber, 1984), pp. 446, 419.

11. Michael Longley, 'Letters' in his *Poems 1963–1983* (Harmondsworth, Penguin, 1986), p. 78.

12. W. J. McCormack, *The Battle of the Books: Two Decades of Irish Cultural Debate* (Gigginstown, The Lilliput Press, 1986), pp. 69, 14.

13. Seamus Heaney, 'Whatever You Say Say Nothing', in *North* (London, Faber and Faber, 1975), p. 60.

14. See Blake Morrison, 'An Expropriated Mycologist', *Times Literary Supplement*, 15 February 1980, 168.

15. John Hewitt, 'For Any Irishman' and 'from Conacre' in Alan Warner, ed., *The Selected John Hewitt* (Belfast, Blackstaff, 1981), pp. 31, 15.

16. Stewart Parker, 'Introduction' in his *Three Plays for Ireland: 'Northern Star', 'Heavenly Bodies', 'Pentecost'* (Birmingham, Oberon Books, 1989), p. 9; and see Seamus Heaney's 'two berserks . . . greaved in a bog, and sinking' in *North*, note 13, p. 70.

17. John Hewitt, note 15, p. 38.

18. Tom Clancy, *Patriot Games* (London, William Collins, 1987).

19. Benedict Kiely, *Proxopera* (London, Quartet Books, 1979).

20. Bernard MacLaverty, *Cal* (London, Jonathan Cape, 1983).

21. Brian Moore, *Lies of Silence* (London, Bloomsbury, 1990).

22. See particularly Paul Muldoon, 'Immram' in his *Why Brownlee Left* (London, Faber and Faber, 1980), pp. 38–47.

23. Robert McLiam Wilson, *Ripley Bogle* (Belfast, Blackstaff, 1989).

24. Danny Morrison, *West Belfast* (Cork, The Mercier Press, 1989).

25. Seamus Deane, *Civilians and Barbarians* (Derry, Field Day, (Pamphlet No. 3), 1983), p. 14.

26. John Montague, *The Rough Field*, 3rd edn. (Dublin, Dolmen, 1979), p. 74.

27. John Hewitt, 'Ulster Names: Postscript 1984', in *Freehold and Other Poems* (Belfast, Blackstaff, 1986), p. 27.

28. Stewart Parker, *Northern Star*, note 16, p. 75.

29. Ciaran Carson, *Belfast Confetti* (Oldcastle, Co. Meath, The Gallery Press, 1989), pp. 72, 66, 11, 69.

30. Seamus Heaney, 'Terminus' in *The Haw Lantern* (London, Faber and Faber, 987), p. 4. See also Paul Muldoon, *Meeting the British* (London, Faber and Faber, 1987) and Tom Paulin, *Fivemiletown* (London, Faber and Faber, 1987).

2

Northern Ireland: a place apart?

George Boyce

Since the Northern Ireland troubles first attracted media attention in the late 1960s, its people, and especially its politics, have
been the subject of sociological, psychological, historical, politically scientific and legal scrutiny, so much so that they could be
forgiven for thinking that they are condemned for ever to live like
specimens in a jar, or like the fly in the fly-bottle, only with no
hope (in their case) of ever escaping from the bottle. Not even the
work of revisionist historians – and history after all is the subject
which is supposed to assist the fly to get out – not even revisionist
historians have budged the stopper one inch. It is probably true,
as George Bernard Shaw remarked, that Ireland is an island
surrounded entirely by footlights.[1] If this is the case, then it may
as well resign itself to the glare of publicity. But it has the right to
ask: what has been the consequence of this great examination?
What light have the footlights thrown on the region, its culture,
its politics, its way of life?

The chief conclusion may be briefly and even simply stated:
Northern Ireland, as conceived by many and probably most of its
observers, is essentially a place apart – an expression used by one
BBC journalist when he stood on a sunny day in July, 1970, and
watched the annual Twelfth parades. The collection of rag, tag
and bobtail youngsters following the processions, in particular,
excited his attention. Watching them, he felt keenly that Northern Ireland was like nowhere else in the world, and certainly
nowhere in the United Kingdom.

It is not hard to see why. Northern Ireland's politics are based
on confrontation and confessionalism, not the bargaining for
social and economic increments that characterises what are called

Jonathan Harris

'British politics'; and it is this mixture of religion and politics that people in Great Britain find particularly odd and offensive. This is natural. The whole of western Europe, let alone Great Britain, has long since moved into a secular society, in which religion occupies the role which modern society assigns to religion – if even that. The Liberal, and then Labour, parties owed much to the English dissenting spirit and tradition; the Conservative Party was once the bastion of Anglicanism. But these are part of what is now regarded as a far-off, arcane past, before the rise of enlightened, modern, secular politics (and enlightened, modern, secular religion).

Violence, too, sets the north of Ireland apart from not only the rest of the British Isles, but the whole of western Europe. Twenty-five years of disorder, murder and terrorism, often of a gratuitous and frenzied kind, categorises Northern Ireland as unique: and the possibility that this violence might bring down the whole apparatus of the state is a serious possibility there, whereas terrorism, in Italy or in West Germany, appears to have little chance of realising its objectives. Certainly it can be said that nowhere else in the United Kingdom sees troops, armoured vehicles and the like deployed regularly on the streets. Nowhere else is a judicial system so altered by violence and the need to fight terrorism. Nowhere else is the judicial system and the police force so much a central part of political controversy.

And all this is part of a central problem, which, again, is apparently without modern parallel in the British Isles or western Europe. This problem is the very legitimacy of the state – the state that used to be (Northern Ireland) and the state of which that region still forms a part (the United Kingdom). The modern federal movement in western Europe emphasises the importance of federalism as a means of preventing the catastrophe of war; and federalists regard terrorism as fundamentally a manageable problem, one which states have shown they can contain, even if they find it hard to eliminate altogether.[2] But the fact that substantial sections of Northern Irish opinion regard the state as itself in question, its historical foundations illegitimate and its political practices since 1922 reprehensible, gives the Northern Ireland problem a volatile element lacking in other cases of terrorism in Europe. The questions of legitimacy and nationalism experienced in Wales or Scotland appear to be but feeble echoes of the intense conflict in the north of Ireland.

It is not only the conflict itself which provokes such reflections:

Ulster people are quick to point out, quite rightly, that the violence is confined to certain, almost predictable, areas, and directly affects the everyday existence of but few people. But the way in which people work within the framework of political instability, sectarianism, and terrorism, or the threat of it, is itself almost uniquely Northern Irish. Rosemary Harris, in her pioneering study,[3] described how people from both sides of the sectarian divide made the necessary accommodations with each other to avoid conflict, disagreement or even just giving offence. Patterns of behaviour emerged and were followed to enable neighbours to live as neighbours for some purposes, and as 'strangers' for other purposes. The subtle nature of the codes of Northern Irish social behaviour, the way in which one side recognised, acknowledged and then lived alongside the other, are part of the way of life of a divided region, but a region with a small, intimate and neighbourly atmosphere – a distinctly Ulster solution to a distinctly Ulster problem. In the troubled atmosphere of post-1968 days, this became even more important, and for the sake of peace it was often essential to live by the method caught by Seamus Heaney in his line, 'Whatever you say, say nothing.'

All this was too much for the instant punditry that emerged after 1968. Guarded neighbourliness, semi-trusting suspicion and friendly doubt placed outside observers at something of a loss and a disadvantage when it came to analysing the Irish North. People who spoke with the same accent, lived in the same kind of houses and streets, looked alike, and yet engaged in often fierce conflict, verbal and real, defied easy explanation. It was small wonder, therefore, that many observers abandoned the effort to understand such a society and turned instead to phenomena which they thought they understood, and which offered ready, if fundamentally inappropriate, parallels. Exotic precedents (Algeria, Cyprus), international conflict (Vietnam), conflicts of colour and race (the southern states of America, South Africa), and even Marxist models (false consciousness in the working class, an aristocracy of labour), all offered at least comforting and familiar guidelines in an otherwise bewildering world. However wildly misleading these may have been, at least they had the merit – in their proponents' eyes – of reinforcing the idea that the conflict was inexplicable in local terms, simply because the local terms were themselves inexplicable.

Northern Ireland, then, was a place apart from the rest of the

United Kingdom. Yet not apart enough. It was, according to some, the result of a kind of almost unholy, and certainly unhappy, sexual encounter between Great Britain and Ireland (or England and Ireland, perhaps). The product of an enforced colonisation of the body (by England); it was, in Heaney's words,

> . . . still; imperially
> Male, leaving you with the pain,
> The rending process in the colony,
> The battering ram, the boom burst from within.

And the consequence was

> . . . an obstinate fifth column
> Whose stance is growing unilateral.[4]

Jonathan Swift's 'injured lady' was thus revived in a more characteristically explicit, almost full-frontal, late twentieth-century image.

All of this may well have an element of truth in it; some of it may even be true. Yet it implies, again, that Northern Ireland is, in the British Isles' experience, unique, apart, the product of the collision – or is it collusion – of native and colonising forces. But whatever the melodramatic nature of the claim, and especially the poetic version of the claim, that Ireland is a 'tracked / And stretchmarked body', it does, inadvertently, point towards an explanation of the Northern Irish predicament, and offer more fruitful ways of understanding and explaining it.

Historians are now more aware of the poverty of the idea of the nation and the nation state as the basic tools of inquiry when they seek to understand the geographical, political and cultural area that is the British Isles. It is, perhaps unsurprisingly, an Irish historian whose interests range more widely than Ireland, who has queried this conceptual misapprehension most effectively and elegantly. Hugh Kearney, in his *The British Isles: A History of Four Nations*,[5] sets aside the claims of 'national' history, and what he calls the 'cage of partial assumptions which lead to the perpetuation of ethnocentric myths and ideologies'. He argues that a 'Britannic framework is an essential starting point for a fuller understanding of these so-called "national" pasts'; and he provides amusing examples of the misapprehensions – including geographical sleights of hand – that the nation-based historical approach invokes: for Sir Lewis Namier 'a great deal of what is peculiar in English history is due to the obvious fact that Great Britain is an island'.[6]

Borders and people have changed since the Roman era – and indeed before that era – and the peoples and states of the British isles, their boundaries and borders, are not what they were hundreds of years ago. This would hardly need saying, were it not for the fact that popular belief would have it otherwise. The nations of Scots, Irish and Welsh might conceivably be regarded as in some sense descending from their forebears, as if immigration and emigration had never taken place. Nations – English or Irish – were seen as having a kind of collective existence, with a memory going back to the distant past (usually when they were more 'free'). And all this is important for an understanding of what is misleading in much of our perception of the Irish North: by stressing 'national history', there is invariably a stress upon the 'difference between a particular society and its neighbours'.[7]

It is not only Professor Kearney who challenges the assumptions which underlie 'national' history; a political scientist, Richard Rose (whose discipline might presuppose him to take national history as a 'model', since 'political science' in the nineteenth century was largely responsible for the creation of the nation-state concept in the first place) also attacked this notion:

> As the people [of Northern Ireland] are a mixture of the descendants of the ancient Irish, plus English and Scottish settlers of the seventeenth century, they could claim to be more typical of the composite British than are the exclusively English people of the Thames valley.[8]

It is arguable, moreover, that this melting-pot effect is more common than might be supposed: the people of South Wales are a mixture of Welsh, English and Irish immigration, now, however, amalgamated in a region and a community with no easily discernible national differences. The people of Wexford are indeed as mixed, racially, as Thomas Davis claimed they were in his celebrated panygeric. Neither of these areas, significantly, is undergoing racial, political or community tensions: national differences, 'Celts' and 'Saxons', or whatever, clearly do not explain the existence of the Northern Irish problem any more than they account for the lack of a South Walian or Wexford problem.

It is more helpful to set aside notions of race and nationality and ask ourselves how best we can study the history, politics and society of a region. Regional history has had an airing recently, even though Ireland lacks – and no doubt will go on lacking – anything comparable to the *Victoria History of the Counties of England*. But regional history all too often breaks down into parochial history, admirable enough in itself, but hardly helpful to anyone who wants to go beyond the farming utensils employed in north Down, or the style of hats worn in County Tyrone at the turn of the century. Regional history has been crushed between the opposite poles of national history (especially the study of central governments) and local history, which does not get beyond the parish pump. Yet regions are vital in an understanding of the history of the British Isles, and especially in understanding the history of the North of Ireland.

Regional history helps us to understand that there exist in the United Kingdom, and the British Isles as a whole, areas whose character is, necessarily, variegated. These areas both show the wider forces that helped to make them what they are, and in turn refract those wider forces, with important local variations, local peculiarities.

Before the nineteenth century, Ulster was regarded as a remote and unimportant part of Ireland and of the British Isles as a whole. Yet it had already participated in a great British enterprise – the plantations of the seventeenth century (as well as the natural process of migration from Scotland and England). And an essential part of this enterprise was the central event in early modern European history – the reformation and counter-reformation, which linked the expansion and influence of the English crown with the fortunes and fate of a biblical reformed religion. The presence in Ulster of an unusually large number of Protestants, and especially Presbyterians, helped give that area its special characteristic; distinctive at least in Ireland, but not so distinctive in a wider British context, since the connections, religious and cultural, between Ulster and the west of Scotland were significant in the eighteenth century, if only because so many Presbyterians went to Scotland for their education. In the nineteenth century the impact of the industrialisation of regions of the British Isles pushed the north of Ireland into economic and political prominence and gave Ulster politics a sharper edge, since to the religious objections to any idea of an Irish 'nation state' were now added important economic arguments. And this brief survey raises a central point in this essay, which is that, as Hugh Kearney points out, whereas 'nations' are supposed to possess a continuity over time, cultures change and interact over time, and the perceptions of one age are not those of another.[9] There is no 'Ulster' mind that can be traced through the centuries: after all, late eighteenth-century Belfast was the centre of liberal and enlightened Presbyterian and Protestant feeling.

The wider forces of British history – the reformation, the expansion of a Protestant people and the efforts to create a British monarchy based on religion, the industrial changes of the nineteenth century – all had a profound impact on Ireland as a whole, and on the north in particular. But the special conditions of Ireland as a whole, and of the north in particular, helped shape and modify the impact of these wider developments.

The politicisation of religion is the obvious point; but because it is obvious, it must not be overlooked. For the process of defining 'Irishness' in the seventeenth century (as Catholic) and its revival in the nineteenth, and then its connection with 'Celticism' in the early twentieth century, meant that whatever 'Irishness' was, Ulster Protestantism was not regarded as an integral part of it. On the contrary, it was easier to define 'Irishness' by saying what it was not, rather than what it was. This again redefined Protestant Ulster, and encouraged and indeed required Protestant Ulster to redefine itself. When Protestant Ulster came to define or redefine itself, it chose the label 'British'; but this again raised problems, since no one then knew precisely what 'Britishness' was, and it still troubles the Ulster Unionist today, only more so, since Britain's population has been altered significantly by large overseas immigration. It is hard (except perhaps for the Provisional IRA) to say who exactly the 'Brits' are whose departure from Ireland is desirable. They are (presumably) white, unlike large sections of the population of contemporary Britain.

The poverty of these descriptions is significant, for it turns our attention to the nature of the society whose character and problems are here considered. The impact of industrialisation provoked a movement of population within the north, with a considerable influx of Roman Catholics from the countryside (especially the post-famine countryside). This changed Belfast from an almost exclusively Protestant city into one with a substantial Roman Catholic minority. Thus the 'outside' event (industrialisation) had a special local impact (the shift in population and the growth of sectarianism). But the two cannot be understood apart. Those who would weep for the secular, enlightened, republican past of late eighteenth-century Belfast[10] would do well to acknowledge that an industrial revolution took place in the British Isles. Similarly, the evangelical movement in nineteenth-century Britain was a common impulse, but in Ireland, and therefore in the North, it had a special edge, since the conversion of souls was, in Irish terms, also the conversion of bodies – voting and political bodies, whose numbers were important in the future of the politics of Ireland and especially the North of Ireland.[11] Changes in the British economy in the nineteenth century encouraged the rise of Belfast as the economic centre of Ireland; and the decline of Dublin[12] again had an important local impact in that it encouraged the idea of a second capital with its future vitally resting on the bosom of the British political and economic system. And to jump forward, the liberal, optimistic, reformist ideas of the 1960s had an impact on the North of Ireland, but one quickly influenced, and modified, by the special local circumstances of the north: the call for civil rights could be seen as an ordinary demand for political change, and therefore an ordinary form of political action. But in the north it was transformed, and not only by Unionists, into a question of Green and Orange (accompanied by the songs of each tradition to speed matters on their way).[13] Similarly, the Sinn Fein-IRA campaign to destabilise Northern Ireland is presented as, and indeed bears the influence of, contemporary anti-colonial struggles; but no one can doubt that it is fuelled by local sectarian feuds, and that it is at best a convenient means of legitimising an impulse of a particular Northern Irish nationalist kind.

When Michael Collins aimed a jibe at the north of Ireland, contrasting it with the 'real' Ireland, and dismissing the Lagan Valley as 'an inferior Lancashire',[14] he was half right, and half wrong; but the bigger half, so to say, was mistaken. The Lagan Valley was not a poor imitation of Lancashire; Lancashire was, rather, a poor imitation of the Lagan Valley. For in Lancashire there existed the same forces that produced conflict in the north of Ireland: the influx of large numbers of people, different in religion from the inhabitants (Catholics from Ireland migrating to industrial Lancashire). The subsequent political and religious tensions were reflected especially in Liverpool, where religion became a dominant political force. This example, alone, would caution us against seeing the north as 'a place apart'. But others are equally significant. Wales has places apart as well: Calvinist Welsh-speaking Wales, industrial anglicised Wales, the Wales of Cardiff – a peculiarly difficult city to place in any recognisable 'national' context. These regions, too, owe much in the making of their character to the forces of reformation, industrialisation, and the idea of 'ethnicity'. Their uncertainty, collectively, on the question of Home Rule is a reflection of the varied and diffuse character of modern Wales.[15]

When Seamus Heaney expostulated against his being identified as a 'British' poet he was, like Michael Collins, half right and half wrong, but the bigger half was wrong. As Edna Longley remarks, 'the technical variety of Ulster poetry, the variety of influences it has absorbed, amount to revisions of twentieth-century literary history too. Irish writing must never be so ghettoised into Irish Studies that it ceases to challenge the assumptions of London, New York and elsewhere'.[16] Again, English influences are transformed and adapted, making non-sense of the idea of national boundaries in literature as in politics: Heaney an Ulster poet, influenced by, but also influencing, English (British?) poetical forms. Culture does not and cannot unify a nation; but it does and can (even when practised by those who reject the consequences of what they are doing) reveal the vital and important fact that nations are not unified things. The region and its environment, the local and the general, ensure that fracture is inescapable, and that in the fractured parts are to be located the unity. For to explore what makes the North what it is involves an exploration of all Britannic cultures and subcultures, and the interaction between them.

It follows, then, that Northern Ireland cannot be seen as, and cannot be, a place apart, for it has been moulded by wider British conditions, and has in turn modified, and sometimes thereby remoulded, the wider British environment. Thus, modern 'Ulster' poetry poses problems, challenges and above all inspiration for those whose field of inquiry is so-called 'English' literature. The northern voice may be special, even unique, but it prevails upon its English audience's attention, and will provoke for English critics the same kind of problems that Yeats, and more especially Joyce, posed for English critics such as F.R. Leavis in their time.[17] (Louis MacNeice posed and poses the same kind of problem, for both Irish and English critics, each of whom wants to shrug him off on the other, since to accept him would cause a redefinition of what 'Irish' and 'English' writing amounts to).[18]

The North of Ireland stands not as a place apart, but rather at a confluence of various, and at times competing, influences and cultures. Because it stands at a confluence, Ulster, to continue the geographical analogy, is shaped by those streams, and yet cannot be said to be merely the result of the combination or mingling of them: the river created by the confluence of other rivers has nonetheless a character of its own, while still retaining the characteristics of its confluent rivers. Its development might seem to take it far away from its origins, as the political experience of modern Northern Ireland seems to do, in contrast with both Great Britain and the rest of Ireland. But this is only to say what everyone acknowledges: that history is about change as well as continuity, and the regions and sub-cultures of the British Isles cannot escape the inexorable logic of the former, any more than they can shrug off the consequences of the latter.

There are, of course, other more obvious points to make about the relationship of the North of Ireland to other parts of the British Isles. As Richard Rose puts it,

> in many respects the peoples of the different parts of the United Kingdom are very similar in their social character-istics, including trade-union membership or weekly earn-ings. Even in Northern Ireland, similarities between Protestants and Catholics greatly outnumber differences.[19]

It needs to be acknowledged immediately that Roman Catholics and Protestants do not share the same job prospects. But the essential truth of Rose's comment is sustained: there is no 'Gaelic', 'Anglican' or 'Presbyterian' life-style that can easily be identified, despite F. S. L. Lyons's brilliant, but ultimately flawed, argument in his *Culture and Anarchy in Ireland*. Roman Catholics and Protestants, of course, have very different percep-tions of themselves, and each other. As Rose explains, the issues at stake in Northern Ireland (and elsewhere in the United Kingdom except parts of Wales) are not about creating different life-styles: the celebrated ice-cream parlours, dance-halls and fish-and-chip shops of Belfast are not, in the event of a Nationalist victory, presumably to be replaced by comely maidens and stalwart young men dancing sets in Donegall Square (the traffic would not allow of it anyway).

The United Kingdom confronts problems of political, economic and social change and identity disputes in an era of disaffection in Scotland and Northern Ireland, and of English adjustment to the dawning awareness that England is not an island, either geo-graphically or – because of the EC – constitutionally. The Republic of Ireland remains singularly free from self-questioning, probably because of its very homogeneity as a state and people. But the fact that politics in the North exhibit the extreme end of the spectrum of 'Britishness' (chauvinistic Union flag waving) and 'Irishness' (chauvinistic tricolour flag waving), naturally predisposes onlookers to see the North as essentially different, apart and entire unto itself (that is, unlike their own contemporary, self-image; the Falklands War and the destruction of the British Embassy in 1972 notwithstanding).

And yet the North of Ireland is a place which, whatever its volatile and violent contemporary politics, despite its political fragmentation, and its clash of identities, offers a kind of epitome of British and Irish history and their cultural and social patterns. The point was put, as long ago as 1963, by Professor J.C. Beckett in his inaugural lecture 'The Study of Irish History'. Professor Beckett drew attention to two major influences which determined the almost inchoate character of Irish history. One was the influence of the land on those who came to live in it from whatever part of the British Isles they originated:

> all were subjected to the same physical influences of life in Ireland, and also to the same social influences which, whether working by repulsion or attraction, affected even those who had no tincture of Gaelic blood. The outlook and traditions they had brought with them were gradually modified; and though they did not wholly cease to be English or Scottish, they became in time Anglo-Irish or (to use an American term) Scotch-Irish.

The other was that

> a large proportion of the settlers resisted complete surrender to the influence of Ireland, and the traditions, ideas and institutions they had imported not only survived, though in modified form, but profoundly affected the earlier population . . . and among the whole Gaelic population a way of life that had been produced by Irish conditions was challenged, and in some measure submerged, by a way of life that had grown up in Britain.[20]

This is true of the whole island of Ireland, as true of Wexford as it is of Antrim. But its working out, with all its tensions and even confrontations, is what makes Northern Ireland not a place apart, but an essential and central part of the whole British and Irish experience.

All this, of course, will not enable the fly to escape from the fly-bottle, but at least it enables it to reflect thoughtfully on the fact that others, besides itself, have contributed to the making of the uncomfortable environment.

References

1. A. T. Q. Stewart, *Edward Carson* (Dublin, 1981), p. 24.
2. This point emerged in a discussion of federalism at a conference organised by the Lothian Foundation in Royal Holloway and Bedford New College, 3–5 April 1989. It was made most forcibly by Professor Lucio Levi of the Fondazione Luigi Einaudi, Turin.
3. Rosemary Harris, *Prejudice and Tolerance in Ulster: A Study of Neighbours and 'Strangers' in a Border Community* (Manchester, 1972).
4. Seamus Heaney 'Act of Union', in *Selected Poems 1965–1975* (London, 1980), pp. 125–6.
5. Hugh Kearney, *The British Isles: A History of Four Nations* (Cambridge University Press), 1989.
6. Kearney, note 5, pp. 1–2.
7. Kearney, note 5, pp. 3–4.
8. Richard Rose, *Governing Without Consensus: An Irish Perspective* (London, 1971), p. 18.
9. Kearney, note 5, p. 8.
10. For example Tom Paulin: see his *Ireland and the English Crisis* (Newcastle, 1984), p. 17.
11. David Hempton, 'The Methodist Crusade in Ireland, 1795–1845', in *Irish Historical Studies*, Vol. XXII, No. 85 (March 1980), 33–48.
12. W. H. Crawford, 'A Look at the Past', in James McLoone, ed., *The British–Irish Connection* (Galway, 1985), pp. 5–6.
13. R. Foster, *Modern Ireland, 1600–1972* (London, 1988), pp. 587–8.
14. D. G. Boyce, *Nationalism in Ireland* (London, 1982), p. 352.
15. For which see *Wales! Wales?* (London, 1984).
16. Edna Longley, 'Including the North', in *Text and Context*, III (Autumn 1988), p. 22.
17. Eamonn Hughes, 'Leavis and Ireland: An Adequate Criticism?', in *Text and Context*, III, pp. 112–32.
18. Tom Paulin, note 10, pp. 75–9.
19. Richard Rose, 'The Constitution: Are we Studying Devolution or Break Up?', in D. Kavanagh and R. Rose, eds., *New Trends in British Politics: Issues for Research* (London, 1977), p. 34.
20. J. C. Beckett, 'The Study of Irish History: An Inaugural Lecture', in *Confrontations: Studies in Irish History* (London, 1972), p. 24.

Wendy Howarth

3

'Why can't you get along with each other?': culture, structure and the Northern Ireland conflict

Joseph Ruane and Jennifer Todd

Introduction

'What is the matter with you – why can't you get along with each other?'[1] This question is guaranteed to infuriate people in Northern Ireland. It implies that the conflict persists simply because they lack the cultural tolerance and maturity to live at peace with each other. It dismisses their view that they face an exceptionally difficult problem, not of their own making, which cannot be solved simply by 'tolerance and maturity'.

The question, and the angry reaction, point to two very different interpretations of the Northern Ireland conflict: they are found as much in the theoretical literature as in popular comment. Those who take the first – the 'cultural' – approach see the source of the conflict in the abnormality of Northern Irish political culture: in the expectations, values, norms and attitudes of the two communities. Those who take the second – the 'structural' – approach see the source of the conflict in the abnormality of the institutional and structural context, in the way that context locks the two communities in conflict.[2]

Those who take the cultural approach argue that the people of Northern Ireland are out of step with contemporary cultural trends. Some emphasise the obsession with extreme and outdated beliefs and attitudes. Each community, it is claimed, is trapped in its ancestral myths, extreme in its nationalism, archaic in its religious beliefs, tribal in its loyalties, intransigent in its political attitudes and prone to violence.[3] Some identify a deeper cultural problem: a degeneration of Christian or moral standards; a narrow essentialist concept of identity and an inability to cope with cultural difference.[4]

Those who take the structural approach argue that the culture of the communities is not abnormal, but the context in which they interact is. Some see it as a 'double minority' problem, whereby the majority in one constitutional arrangement would be the minority in another.[5] Others have pointed to more specific issues: the permanent unionist majority which makes British-style parliamentary democracy unworkable; or the obstacles to consociational democracy in the Northern Ireland context.[6] Some emphasise the structural relations within and between the two communities in Northern Ireland, some the structural relations within Ireland, some the totality of relations within the British Isles, and some the international context.[7]

Different policy emphases follow from each approach. When the problem is defined as a cultural one, the solution is sought in education, exhortation and the reconciliation of traditions. When the problem is defined structurally, the solution is sought in institutional reform or constitutional change. Up to the present, these two approaches have not been clearly distinguished. Yet almost every commentator takes one or other approach. The balance of opinion changes over time and is closely related to political events. In the period before the signing of the Anglo-Irish Agreement, a structural interpretation was predominant: the central problem was defined as an imbalance of power and rights between the two communities in Northern Ireland. Those who framed the Agreement saw it as a solution to that problem. The continuation of conflict since the Agreement has led to a re-emphasis on cultural causes: if the 'framework for a solution' is now present, the persistence of conflict must be due to the unreasonableness and intransigence of the two sides.

In this essay we argue that the conflict has structural rather than cultural roots, and that the structural problem is much deeper than is commonly recognised. We argue that, in a comparative perspective, Northern Irish political culture is not unusual. The overt signs of conflict – bigotry and intransigence – arise because the communities' fundamental interests are incompatible within Northern Ireland as it is presently structured.

This situation is constituted and reproduced by socio-political relations which transcend the boundaries of Northern Ireland. As such, the problem is beyond the power of the people of Northern Ireland to resolve. Institutional mechanisms such as the Anglo-Irish Agreement do not deal with the underlying causes of the conflict. It can only be resolved by an extensive and radical restructuring of the British and/or Irish states.

Culture or structure?

According to the cultural view, the roots of the conflict in Northern Ireland lie in a cluster of abnormal and problematic values, beliefs and attitudes. These include: an obsession with the past conceived in mythical terms, extreme nationalism, religious intolerance, an unwillingness to compromise and a willingness to use or condone political violence. Each side is said to be in a timewarp, out of touch with present-day reality, entrapped in a mythical view of the past which leads to endless repetition of old tribal conflicts. They are preoccupied with nationalist concerns – identity, boundaries, sovereignty – now universally agreed to be irrelevant to real material problems in an increasingly international world. They are unique in the Western world in their religious intolerance and their refusal to move beyond sectarian prejudices more appropriate to the sixteenth than the twentieth century. Each side is unrelenting in its determination to achieve its goals and to achieve absolute victory over the other. Each side directly uses, or colludes in, violence to achieve its goals.[8]

This description of Northern Ireland's political culture is often treated as obvious – 'just look at what those people say and do'. But abnormal political preoccupations and behaviour do not necessarily indicate an abnormal political culture. As we argue below, they may be a response to abnormal structural conditions. It is held that people in Northern Ireland are unusually preoccupied with the past, and, more precisely, with a mythic version of it.[9] This view is questionable. All modern societies tell and retell their pasts; their cultures are pervaded with myths about past defeats and victories, the ways of life of previous generations and the origins of the society, its distinctive cultures, its national customs and institutions and its present inequalities.[10] These myths are embedded in the popular culture; many are publicly and ritually celebrated on a regular basis.

Northern Ireland is unusual in that so many of its myths stress conflict and division. Elsewhere the dominant myths stress harmony and integration. Those societies have myths of conflict and division, but typically their harshest and most divisive myths are reserved for vanquished enemies or neighbouring societies with which they have had a long history of conflict.[11] The prevalence of myths of conflict in Northern Ireland does not, however, indicate an attraction to, or entrapment in, such myths. It arises from the fact that Northern Ireland brings together, in a situation that encourages conflict and competition, two groups with allegiances to two different national communities which themselves have a long history of conflict. Myths of past conflict and division offer explanations and justifications for present conflict; they are not indulged in for their own sake. In fact, people in Northern Ireland readily ignore the dominant conflictual myths when structural conditions permit. In local communities, Protestant-Catholic co-operation and integration in everyday life are accompanied by myths of integration, decency and 'the one blood'.[12] That this process does not take place at the societal level is a product of the distinctive social structure of Northern Ireland, not its culture.

The cultural view points to the preoccupation with national identity, culture, boundaries and sovereignty in Northern Ireland, and attributes it to an extreme form of cultural nationalism. However, other Western states and populations have similar preoccupations. They invest major resources to maintain their 'national interest', 'national territory' and 'national culture'. If these are threatened, there is intense state and public concern. This is evident in the response of the United States in the wake of the defeat in Vietnam, English attitudes during the Falklands war, France's concern about its language and culture in an increasingly Anglophone world, and Canada's concern about cultural domination by a larger neighbour.

Moreover, the main political parties in Northern Ireland have thoroughly reformulated and modernised their positions on these issues in recent years. The SDLP has deconstructed the notion of the Irish nation; it focuses on people rather than territory; it speaks of a legacy of conflict which must be transcended in a wider European context.[13] Mainstream Unionist intellectuals continually update their views in line with contemporary trends and have much in common with state-centred, technocratic elites throughout the modern world.[14] Sinn Fein too has undergone considerable transformation. The traditionalist romantic rhetoric of the early 1970s has given way to a more secular and rational approach.[15] Old-fashioned Irish, Ulster and British nationalists exist but they are a minority, and similar types exist in all Western countries.[16]

There is intense public concern about issues concerning identity and culture, boundaries and sovereignty in Northern Ireland. But the level of concern is, for the most part, a product of structural conditions, not of old-fashioned cultural nationalism. Northern Ireland as a political entity is unstable, 'suspended' between the United Kingdom and the Republic of Ireland, with an uncertain future. Any change in its constitutional status would have crucial implications for each community. Their concern with constitutional issues is not a romantic cultural distraction from 'real', 'bread and butter' issues, but an expression of real material interests. These include political interests in the locus of political power and the networks through which it will be exercised, economic interests for those groups and regions which will benefit from one or other constitutional arrangement, and interests in retaining control of cultural resources. It is this, rather than some archaic attachment to traditional nationalism, which lies behind the preoccupation with national boundaries, sovereignty and identity in Northern Ireland.

The cultural view points to the sharp and bitter religious divide and to examples of sectarianism and religious intolerance. This, it is claimed, is proof of the cultural distinctiveness and pathology of Northern Ireland. However, Northern Ireland is not so distinctive in this regard. Each of its religious communities has counterparts elsewhere which share its basic beliefs and many of its prejudices. The recent reactions of some Scandinavian Protestant clergy to the Pope's visit illustrate that Northern Irish Protestants are not unique in Europe in their fear of Papal power. The extent of religious practice and belief is high in comparison with many other Western countries, but religiosity as such does not mean intolerance. Nor indeed is religious intolerance as prevalent in Northern Ireland as some well-publicised events suggest.

Religion does impinge on the political domain to an unusual degree in Northern Ireland, and sectarianism is a reality, but this too is a product of structural conditions. First, the religious divide coincides with the cultural, political and ethnic/national divide.

As a result, political and national conflict is aggravated by the religious opposition, and vice versa. Second, Northern Ireland is constitutionally unstable. It lies between two states each of which has a very different religious ethos: the British state is steeped in Protestantism (though now in a fairly secular form), and the Republic, despite its formal division of church and state, is steeped in Roman Catholicism. Constitutional change would have major consequences for the religious communities. Northern Protestants are particularly concerned; they believe that membership of the United Kingdom is a condition of their survival as a community with a distinctive religious ethos, and that integration into an unreconstructed Republic would threaten their communal survival. It is the indeterminacy of the situation and the consequences of any change in it that make religion so important.

If Northern Irish people are not distinctive in the content of their views, are they distinctive in the way they pursue them? According to the cultural interpretation, the conflict persists because neither community is willing to compromise. Each side insists on total victory: unionists want an entirely British Northern Ireland, nationalists want an entirely Irish Ireland.[17] It is true that neither side compromises enough to reach political agreement, but there is little evidence of a generalised cultural trait of intransigence among Northern Irish people. On the contrary, they compromise readily in most areas of social life, from industrial to interpersonal relations. Unwillingness to compromise is limited to one area only – the constitutional question – and even in this area it is not absolute. Moreover, the communities in Northern Ireland are less distinctive in this regard than is frequently acknowledged. No modern Western society readily yields on constitutional issues. The reluctance to compromise on the constitutional question in Northern Ireland is so strong because of the structural context in which compromise is required. Too much is at stake: issues of fundamental material, political, cultural and religious rights. The fact that the future lies in the balance makes compromise all the more difficult, for if one side shows itself too willing it may irretrievably damage its bargaining position.

Finally, the cultural view emphasises the tolerance of political violence in Northern Ireland. This is contrasted with other European examples of historical enemies now resolving their differences by peaceful means. That the two communities in

Northern Ireland are unwilling to disown totally the 'men of violence' is seen as a failure of moral development or as deep cultural pathology. At its crudest this is the view that the (Northern) Irish are 'a people who love killing, they like living in hell, they enjoy their incomprehensible quarrel, they are nothing to do with us.'[18]

Northern Irish attitudes to violence are less distinctive than they may first appear. Few individuals in any society, and no major states, are pacifist. Force is held to be legitimate in defending a legitimately constituted state, in repulsing armed aggression and in situations where agreed institutions for re-solving disputes do not exist. Those who use violence in Northern Ireland justify it in terms of the same moral and political principles that other Western societies use.[19] The security forces argue that they are applying the law in the face of terrorism; loyalist paramilitaries argue that they must defend their basic rights because the legitimate authority – the British state – is unable or unwilling to do this; republicans argue that British rule in Ireland is illegitimate and draw on 'just war' theory to justify their challenge to it. The use of violence in Northern Ireland is tragic, reprehensible and futile, but it is not distinctive either in form or in justification. There are certainly individuals in North-ern Ireland, as in all societies, whose use of violence is an expression of personal pathology; but there is no basis for attributing such pathology to all who use it, or to the culture of their community.[20] In short, the conflict is not a product of cultural abnormality. The distinctiveness of Northern Irish politi-cal culture has been much exaggerated. In its ideologies and its underlying culture, Northern Ireland is an integral part of the contemporary world and shares the basic features of modern Western culture. If we are to understand the source of the conflict we must look not for cultural peculiarities but for structural conditions which make conflict so difficult to avoid.

The structural basis of conflict

We have argued that the conflict in Northern Ireland is a product of structural not cultural factors. What are these factors and how do they contribute to the conflict? Are they within the control of the people of Northern Ireland? The nature of the conflict and its intractability arise out of a complex and interlocking set of relationships: some between the two communities in Northern

Ireland, some between each community and the United Kingdom and the Republic of Ireland, and some within and between these two societies. Such a structural configuration led to the foundation of Northern Ireland as a distinct entity. It has conditioned the community conflict ever since. It underpins a situation in which the fundamental interests of one community can be secured only at the expense of the fundamental interests of the other. The two communities in Northern Ireland are caught in a structural bind. This bind is maintained and stabilised by forces that transcend the boundaries of Northern Ireland.

As is well known, Northern Ireland was founded in the context of Irish nationalist struggle against British rule. Ulster unionists feared that they would be materially deprived and politically and culturally marginalised in an independent Ireland. The British government backed their demands for exclusion from an Irish state and established Northern Ireland as a distinct but integral part of the United Kingdom with a devolved government responsible for its internal affairs.[21] A third of the population of the new Northern state was Catholic and nationalist, bitterly opposed to the settlement. The Northern state was permanently unstable. It was no one's first choice and its existence and boundaries could not easily be legitimated. The disaffected nationalist minority within Northern Ireland was large enough to threaten the existence of the state. Its legitimacy was not recognised by the new state in the South. The British state initially saw it as transitory. Its commitment to Northern Ireland has always been subject to wider international interests and pressures.[22]

Community relations within Northern Ireland developed according to the logic of the situation. Unionists monopolised political, economic and cultural power, and controlled the channels of communication with Westminster. They built a society which was overwhelmingly Protestant and British, although in a specific Ulster version. They constructed a mythology of the distant and proximate origins of their state, its foundation and subsequent development.[23] They proudly compared their society, with its British ethos and higher standard of living, to the South. It was their state, created to secure their interest on the island.

From the start, nationalists refused to recognise the legitimacy of the Northern state. Unionists excluded them from any share in the state and discriminated against them economically, politically and culturally. The repressive forces of the state were used to stabilise this situation.[24] They justified their actions on the grounds of nationalist disloyalty. More fundamentally, however, the kind of state which unionists set out to build could not have accommodated nationalists on an equal basis: its institutions and ethos were to be predominantly British and Protestant. Catholics became a marginalised and repressed minority in a state which they felt should not have existed in the first place. The political mobilisation for civil rights in the late 1960s brought into the open the deeply conflicting interests of the two communities. It brought the British state back as a direct actor in the situation, involved the government of the Republic, and exposed Northern Ireland to international scrutiny. The subsequent partial restructuring of Northern Ireland did not, however, fundamentally change the conditions which led to community conflict.

Direct British involvement has reduced some of the structural imbalance between the two communities. With the abrogation of Stormont, the unionist monopoly of power has gone. Most of the overtly discriminatory institutions have been reformed, but at a deeper level structural inequality remains.[25] The western, largely Catholic, part of the province is economically underdeveloped while the Catholic unemployment rate is significantly higher than the Protestant throughout Northern Ireland. A unionist ethos prevails at the higher levels of state institutions and nationalist views are politically marginalised. The local security forces remain predominantly Protestant and gross breaches of civil liberties continue to occur. British culture has clear predominance over Irish in the public domain.

The community conflict has been fought out in this new structural context. The nationalist sense of grievance remains strong.[26] Relatively few are satisfied with the formal legal and political equality which has already been achieved. Some demand economic equality and reform of the security forces within Northern Ireland. Some want real power, not just formal political equality. Some add to this the demand for equality of the two cultural and national traditions. Some want much more: an immediate withdrawal of the British state from Ireland and the formation of a united Ireland. But, for most, full equality within Northern Ireland – including substantive economic equality and equality of power and status – is the present goal.

Unionists have always resisted nationalist demands for full equality. Their resistance is based on two considerations. First, it would involve them in immediate sacrifices. Without economic development, economic equality would mean a decline of Protestant living standards, particularly among the working class.[27] Political equality would mean unionists giving up their rights as the majority for whom Northern Ireland was originally created. They would have to share power with a community whose goals, interests and ethos differ fundamentally from their own. Cultural equality would mean that a British ethos would no longer predominate in Northern Ireland. Unionists' status in what they consider 'their own society' would be greatly reduced and, for some, destroyed.

Secondly, and more importantly, full equality in Northern Ireland would, unionists believe, place its very existence at risk. It would reduce their own power and status relative to nationalists, weaken unionist solidarity and reduce their ability to defend their position. Unionists still think that their incorporation into a united Ireland would mean certain material impoverishment, political and cultural marginalisation, and ultimate extinction as a community. Their opposition to equality reflects to an important degree their fear that it would be the first step on this road. In this context, nationalist insistence on a formal role for the Republic in Northern Ireland simply confirms unionist fears that equality will lead to Dublin rule. For unionists, equality with nationalists is incompatible with their own security.

The communities in Northern Ireland are therefore caught in a structural bind. In the logic of the situation neither side can yield without sacrificing its fundamental interests: for unionists, security; for nationalists, equality. As long as these conditions obtain, the conflict is self-perpetuating and irresolvable. No amount of dialogue, tolerance and search for reconciliation can overcome it. Nor can violence. Republican violence deepens unionist fears; state repression and loyalist violence intensify nationalist grievances. The structural bind is internal to Northern Ireland. Unionists and nationalists, by their actions, reinforce inequality and insecurity. But they feel compelled to do this because their situation offers no other way to defend their interests. Their actions are conditioned by a context over which they have little control. The context is defined by the two states, their internal structures and the relations between them.

The British state is an elaborate, internally differentiated, economic, political and cultural power structure, centralised and centralising.[28] The centres of power are located in the south-east of England, historically the core region of the British Isles, and once the centre of a vast imperial system. The internal hierarchical structure of the British Isles developed in tandem with the construction of empire and, to a large extent, has survived its demise.[29] Social and cultural inequalities within the United Kingdom today are deep-rooted and pervasive, among classes, regions, nations and ethnic groups. Struggle against inequality and privilege has brought about some progressive legislation and a welfare state. But it has not seriously challenged traditional social and territorial power structures.[30]

Structural inequality in the United Kingdom as a whole creates major impediments to the achievement of equality between Protestants and Catholics in Northern Ireland. Northern Ireland is at once a local form of the United Kingdom's hierarchical structure and a subordinated unit within it. The achievement of economic equality between Protestant and Catholic would require the commitment of an unprecedented level of resources to Northern Ireland, but resources are scarce; the United Kingdom has many marginal and deprived regions, and commitment to regional redistribution is limited.[31] Full political equality for nationalists would require power-sharing and a higher degree of devolution, decentralisation and democratisation than is compatible with the British state's central control of key policy areas.[32] The achievement of cultural equality in Northern Ireland is hindered by the deeply rooted hierarchical character of the British cultural system which ranks Ulster-British higher than Irish culture.[33] The difficulty of keeping the problems of Northern Irish Catholics on the British political agenda reflects the low status of Northern Ireland in the United Kingdom. In short, the centralised and hierarchical structure of the United Kingdom underpins the inequality of Catholics in Northern Ireland and sets clear limits to what the British government can do to remedy this.

The Republic of Ireland is a profoundly different kind of state. It is recent in origin, small in scale and economically peripheral. It came into being as a result of a nationalist and anti-imperialist struggle that sought the independence of the island as a whole from Great Britain. Irish unity, though not actively pursued, remains a popular aspiration and is enshrined in the Constitution. Although not culturally homogenous – regional differences are important – the Republic is religiously and ethnically so. Its ethos is Catholic and nationalist; the power of the Catholic Church and of nationalist organisations, though increasingly questioned, remains strong.[34] Those who dissent from that ethos are marginalised. There are strong egalitarian elements to its culture, but there is a clear internal class and power structure.[35] Class divisions are strong, and the working class is weakly organised. There is considerable poverty and little progressive legislation. Economic, political and cultural power are highly centralised and centred on Dublin.[36] The Republic as a state reflects the traditions of Southern Ireland, not the island as a whole.

The present structure of the Republic of Ireland is an impediment to the resolution of the conflict. Unionists' fear of Irish unity underpins and legitimates their resistance to reform within Northern Ireland. Unity is rejected on economic grounds since it would mean a fall in living standards. But it is rejected on other grounds too: the power of the Catholic Church, the lack of progressive social legislation and respect for minority rights, the Southern focus and Dublin-centredness of the power elite and of the society as a whole, and the dominance of the Gaelic-Nationalist tradition. Hostility to unity is further intensified by the failure of the Republic to demonstrate a clear commitment to the building of an island-wide society which would respect Protestant and unionist traditions. The Republic's expressed aspiration to unity and its claim to jurisdiction over Northern Ireland exacerbate unionist concerns but are not their source. It is the possibility of unity that most threatens unionists. Even were the Republic to remove the claim and change its aspirations, the possibility of unity would remain, however remote. As long as the Republic retains its present structure, unionists will fear and resist unity and will also resist reforms within Northern Ireland which might open the way to it.[37]

The Anglo-Irish Agreement of 1985 gave to the Republic the right and responsibility to act as spokesparty for the nationalist community in Northern Ireland. The pace of reforms has, however, been much slower than was initially anticipated. In part, this is because the nature of the relationship between the British and Irish states undermines the Republic's ability to fulfil its role. Each state is sovereign and independent and in theory equal to the other. But the Republic is an ex-colony of Britain, with a fraction of its population and economic and military resources. It is lower in cultural esteem and in international standing and influence. It has, moreover, interests of its own. It wishes to maintain good relations with the United Kingdom and is unwilling to endanger them by pressing Northern nationalists' demands too insistently. Its capacity to fulfil its role under the terms of the Anglo-Irish Agreement is therefore limited. Under present conditions, pressure from the Republic will not be sufficient to establish equality for nationalists within Northern Ireland.

In summary, the conflict is generated by a structural bind within Northern Ireland which is reproduced and stabilised outside its boundaries, by the internal structures and mutual relations of the two sovereign states. Nationalists have a fundamental interest in equality which is blocked not just by unionist resistance but by the internal structures of the British state itself: the union, in its present form, stabilises nationalist inequality. Unionists have a fundamental interest in security which is threatened by the very proximity of an unreconstructed Republic. They have attempted to defend their community through the union with Britain: greater equality with nationalists removes their defences against Irish unity. Under present circumstances, one community's fundamental interest can be secured only at the expense of the other's. Appeals to tolerance, understanding and liberal values have little effect; such principles offer no way of resolving such fundamental conflicts of interest. If the Northern Ireland conflict is to be resolved, it has to be addressed at the wider level of the structures of the two states and the relationship between them.

Conclusion

For many writers the roots of the Northern Ireland conflict lie in the anachronistic ideas and ideals, mistaken perceptions or exaggerated fears of the people of Northern Ireland. We have argued that this idealist position mistakes the cultural expressions and manifestations of the conflict for its deep causes. It subjectivises the conflict and supposes that a change of ideas and perceptions will resolve it. It ignores its structural basis. Even descriptively, the cultural approach is mistaken. Northern Irish culture deviates little from mainstream Western culture on such issues as myth, nationalism, religion, compromise and violence. The basic motivations and interests which sustain conflict are not romantic nationalism or sixteenth-century theology, but concerns with equality, security and the distribution of power. In other words, ordinary liberal-democratic concerns produce conflict in the structural context of Northern Ireland. The roots of the conflict lie in actual social relationships, not in perceptions. The conflict is ultimately about conflicting interests, not conflicting ideas. It arises because the structure of the situation is such as to place the two communities in a bind in which their fundamental interests are irreconcilably opposed. It is not in their power to change these conditions. The dominant structural relations – those which maintain and intensify the bind – are not located within Northern Ireland but within and between Britain and the Republic. To ignore the real structural determinants of the conflict, and to suppose some cultural abnormality in the people of Northern Ireland is to displace responsibility for the conflict.

References

1. The topic of this paper, and many of the ideas in it, owe much to interviews with Northern Protestants and Catholics conducted by the authors in the summer of 1988.
2. The distinction between the two approaches lies in the method used, not in the content discussed. It is possible to give cultural explanations of institutional developments, and social-structural explanations of cultural phenomena.
3. For example, a recent television programme was entitled 'The sixteenth century is alive and well and living in Northern Ireland'. RTE 1, Radharc, transmitted 23 May 1989.
4. 'Tribalism and Christianity in Ireland' (New Ulster Movement Publications, 1973); Roy F. Foster, 'Varieties of Irishness', in M. Crozier, ed., *Cultural Traditions in Northern Ireland* (Belfast, Institute of Irish Studies, 1989), p. 22.
5. For a discussion, see John Whyte, 'Interpretations of the Northern Ireland Problem: An Appraisal', *Economic and Social Review*, Vol. 9, No. 4 (1978), 257–282.
6. New Ulster Movement, 'Reform of Stormont' (NUM publications, 1971). Arend Lipjhart, 'Consociation: The Model and its Applications in Divided Societies' in Desmond Rea, ed., *Political Cooperation in Divided Societies* (Dublin, Gill and Macmillan, 1982), pp. 183–4.
7. Examples include: Frank Wright, *Northern Ireland: A Comparative Analysis* (Dublin, Gill and Macmillan, 1987); Kevin Boyle and Tom Hadden, *Ireland: A Positive Proposal* (Harmondsworth, Penguin, 1985); Adrian Guelke, *Northern Ireland: The International Perspective* (Dublin, Gill and Macmillan, 1988).
8. New Ulster Movement, note 4, provides a coherent statement of this

position. For examples of a wide range of authors who hold such views, see The Two Traditions Group, 'Northern Ireland and the Two Traditions in Ireland' (Belfast, Two Traditions Group, 1983), pp. 13–16.

9. John Magee in *Cultural Traditions in Northern Ireland*, note 4, p. 36. See also: New Ulster Movement, note 4; Henry Grant SJ, 'Understanding the Northern Irish Troubles: A Preliminary to Action', *Studies* (Summer 1983), 1–17.

10. For a valuable discussion, see R. V. Comerford, 'Political Myths in Modern Ireland' in Princess Grace Library, ed., *Irishness in a Changing Society* (Buckinghamshire, Colin Smythe, 1988), pp. 1–17.

11. Such myths perform socially integrating functions. See Frank Wright note 7, pp. 20–27.

12. Elliott Leyton, 'Opposition and Integration in Ulster', *Man*, Vol. 9 (1974), 185–98, p. 194; A. D. Buckley, *A Gentle People: A Study of a Peaceful Community in Ulster* (Cultra, Ulster Folk and Transport Museum, 1982); Aileen Cronin, 'War and Peace: A Study of Hostility and Harmony in Northern Ireland', MA thesis, Department of Politics, University College Dublin (1989).

13. See John Hume's interview with Frank Millar, *Irish Times* (13 January 1989) for a recent statement of the SDLP position.

14. For example, R. L. McCartney, 'Liberty and Authority in Ireland', *Field Day pamphlet No. 9* (Derry, Field Day, 1985); Arthur Aughey, *Under Siege: Ulster Unionism and the Anglo–Irish Agreement* (Belfast, Blackstaff, 1989); Tom Wilson, *Ulster: Conflict and Consent* (Oxford, Basil Blackwell, 1989).

15. A comparison of *Republican News* of the early 1970s with *An Phoblacht/Republican News* today shows this clearly. The change occurred in the mid-1970s.

16. In interviews we found little evidence of traditionalist nationalist attitudes. They may indeed be less common in Northern Ireland than elsewhere because the conflict, public debate, and glare of world attention have forced many people to a more critical and reflective stance.

17. Cahal Daly, 'Towards a New Society in which Every Person has a Place', paper presented at a conference, 'Northern Ireland: Finding a Way Forward', at the Corrymeela Centre, Ballycastle, 8 October 1988. Two Traditions Group, note 8, pp. 10–12.

18. Thus Charles Moore describes the 'instinctive British feeling about the Irish', *Irish Times* (5 April 1988).

19. Guelke, note 7, chapter 2.

20. See Ken Heskin, *Northern Ireland: A Psychological Analysis* (Dublin, Gill and Macmillan, 1980), chapter 4. Heskin, 'The Psychology of Terrorism in Northern Ireland' in Yonah Alexander and Alan O'Day, eds., *Terrorism in Ireland* (London, Croom Helm, 1984), pp. 88–105.

21. For the formal and informal constraints on the devolved government, see Patrick Buckland, *The Factory of Grievances: Devolved Government in Northern Ireland 1921–1939* (Dublin, Gill and Macmillan, 1979), pp. 9–77.

22. For a discussion of these issues in the early years, see Dennis Kennedy, *The Widening Gulf: Northern Attitudes to the Independent Irish State* (Belfast, Blackstaff, 1988).

23. For a coherent statement of this mythology, see Rev. Ian R. K. Paisley, Peter D. Robinson and John D. Taylor, *Ulster – the Facts* (Belfast, Crown Publications, 1982).

24. John Whyte, 'How Much Discrimination was there under the Unionist Regime, 1921–1968?' in T. Gallagher and J. O'Connell, eds., *Contemporary Irish Studies* (Manchester, Manchester University Press, 1983), pp. 1–35; Michael Farrell, 'The Apparatus of Repression', *Field Day pamphlet No. 11* (Derry, Field Day, 1986).

25. Bill Rolston, 'Reformism and Sectarianism: The State of the Union after Civil Rights', in John Darby, ed., *Northern Ireland: The Background to the Conflict* (Belfast, Appletree, 1983), pp. 197–224; John Darby, 'Reform? An assessment of political, administrative and institutional changes in Northern Ireland since 1969', *L'Irelande Politique et Sociale/Ireland: Politics and Society*, Vol. 1, No. 3 (1987), 13–25. On economic inequality, see Liam O'Dowd, 'Trends and Potential of the Service Sector in Northern Ireland' and Frank Gafikin and Mike Morrissey, 'Poverty and Politics in Northern Ireland', in Paul Teague, ed., *Beyond the Rhetoric: Politics, the Economy and Social Policy in Northern Ireland* (London, Lawrence and Wishart, 1987), pp. 183–210, 136–159.

26. J. Ruane and J. Todd, 'Commonality and Difference in the Views of Northern Catholics', paper presented to joint sessions, European Consortium of Political Research, Paris, April 1988.

27. Under present conditions, this would mean absolute poverty. See Gafikin and Morrissey, note 25.

28. For an overview, see David Coates, *The Context of British Politics* (London, Hutchinson, 1984). On the economic level, see Ron Martin, 'The Political Economy of Britain's North-South Divide' in Jim Lewis and Alan Townsend, eds., *The North-South Divide: Regional Change in Britain in the 1980s* (London, Paul Chapman, 1989), pp. 20–60. On the cultural level, see John Osmond, *The Divided Kingdom* (London, Constable, 1988). On the political level, for two different perspectives, see Jim Bulpitt, *Territory and Power in the United Kingdom: An Interpretation* (Manchester, Manchester University Press, 1983) and Richard Rose, *Understanding the United Kingdom: The Territorial Dimension in Government* (London, Longman, 1982).

29. Jim Bulpitt, 'The Making of the United Kingdom: Aspects of English Imperialism', *Parliamentary Affairs* (Spring 1987), 174–189 and Bulpitt, note 28, chapter 3; Angus Calder, *Revolutionary Empire: The Rise*

of the English Speaking Empires from the 15th Century to the 1780s (New York, E. P. Dutton, 1981); Tom Nairn, *The Break-Up of Britain: Crisis and Neo-Nationalism* (London, Verso, 1977), chapter 1.

30. Martin, note 28, pp. 49–51; Nairn, note 29, pp. 47–52; Osmond, note 28, pp. 193–5.

31. Rose, note 28, pp. 96–101, and chapter 6.

32. Cf. Bulpitt, note 28, pp. 222, and Rose, note 28, pp. 110–15.

33. See Osmond, note 28, chapters 1, 6 and 7 on the British cultural hierarchy.

34. On the power of the Catholic church, see Tom Inglis, *Moral Monopoly: The Catholic Church in Modern Irish Society* (Dublin, Gill and Macmillan, 1987).

35. Michel Peillon, *Contemporary Irish Society: An Introduction* (Dublin, Gill and Macmillan, 1982); Chris Eipper, *The Ruling Trinity: A Community Study of Church, State and Business in Ireland* (Aldershot, Gower, 1986); Christopher T. Whelan and Brendan J. Whelan, 'Social Mobility in the Republic of Ireland: A Comparative Perspective', ESRI paper No. 116, (July 1984).

36. Joseph Lee, 'Centralisation and Community' in Joseph Lee, ed., *Ireland: Towards a Sense of Place* (Cork, Cork University Press, 1985), pp. 84–101.

37. Some argue that Northern Protestants will fear and resist Irish unity under any circumstances because they are British and would find it wholly unacceptable to live in an Irish state. For one such argument see John A. Murphy, 'Religion and Irish Identity' in the Princess Grace Library, ed., note 10, pp. 138–9. These arguments do not accurately reflect the complexity of, and variation within, Northern Protestant cultural identity and political concerns.

Ben Clowes

4

Cuchullain and an RPG-7: the ideology and politics of the Ulster Defence Association

James W. McAuley

They [the paramilitaries] are as representative of their community as any other more acceptable institution. If they represent a dark side to the nature of that community then it is because that side exists within the community and within the individuals who belong to it. . . . We ignore at our peril the particularity of their origin, and of their development, which in fact determines their existence.[1]

Introduction

Since the early 1970s paramilitary organisations have provided an important channel for articulating both social grievances and for reproducing sectarian ideology within the Protestant working class (PWC hereafter) in Northern Ireland. By far the most influential in terms of visibility and activity are the Ulster Defence Association (UDA) and the Ulster Volunteer Force (UVF). The origins and development of the latter have been discussed elsewhere.[2] This paper will concentrate on the activities of the largest of these organisations, the UDA, membership of which remains legal, unlike that of the UVF. While it is not the intention to minimise those activities by the UDA which have taken the form of 'military' actions against the Catholic population, such actions do not fully explain the reasons for the formation, or the continued existence, of the UDA. This paper will therefore also discuss the political development of the organisation and suggest reasons why these parallel directions have evolved.

The form of the two major directions within the UDA were clearly illustrated by recent editions of the organisation's monthly magazine *Ulster*. The March 1989 edition featured on its cover a photograph of Michael Stone, the loyalist gunman who attacked mourners at the funeral of an IRA member at Miltown Cemetery. Under the headline 'Our Man Flint: Loyalist hero Michael Stone – against all odds', the editorial lamented that Ulster was 'short of similar heroes' and that loyalists had a 'penchant for "jaw-jaw" instead of "war-war"'.[3] The editorial of the next edition, April 1989, however, was given to the organisation's political wing, the Ulster Loyalist Democratic Party (ULDP). The editorial denounced the 'Loyalist unity' created by Ian Paisley and James Molyneaux, as a 'smokescreen for inaction, doubt and prevarication' and declared the ULDP's aims as 'seeking a mandate for the creation of a truly representative and democratic government'.[4] How have these parallel strategies developed? To explain this it is first necessary to outline the local social structure within which the organisation developed.

Local social structure and sectarianism

Sectarian ideology and its reproduction is an essential element in the culture of both nationalist and unionist blocs in Northern Ireland. This culture of sectarianism is most clearly identified within the working class. It is strengthened by the level of physical segregation and each community's ignorance of the other's life patterns. Such divisions are well established in working-class culture in Belfast. Here, Harbinson describes his experience of loyalist attitudes in the late 1950s:

> Our ignorance of the Catholic world was profound. I, for instance, believed that Mickeys existed only in parts of Belfast and nowhere else except the Free State and Rome itself. That many Catholics were living in London, or were allowed to live in London with our Protestant King seemed impossible.[5]

Boyd gives a similar example of his socialisation into the easy acceptance of communal division:

> 'Fight for Billy, Fight for Billy, Fight for the Cock o' the North!' That was one of our best songs, and we used to shout

it at the top of our voices as we paraded along the smelly back entries in defiance of the Catholics who were preparing to attack us. That none of us had ever seen a Catholic or knew anything about the 'Cock of the North' didn't matter in the least. Somewhere near us there was a big fight going on and we Protestants wanted to be on the winning side.[6]

Sectarianism is central to an understanding of the social relations of loyalism and to an understanding of day-to-day life in loyalist areas of Belfast. In its contemporary form sectarianism is located in a strength of common identity and high levels of social segregation. Loyalist Belfast is cemented by traditions based on a common history. This history is highly selective (as of course is 'republican history'). Several commentators have pointed to the way in which 'history' is put to use in everyday life.[7] As Rose has suggested, 'Ireland is almost a land without history because the troubles of the past are relived as contemporary events.'[8]

Sectarianism also manifests itself in high levels of physical segregation. The traditional loyalist working-class community was densely populated and in many cases practically self-contained.[9] The social structure of such communities was organised around the extended family, close friendship networks, geographical stability and cultural homogeneity.[10]

This 'sectarian socialisation' is, however, not all-embracing. The development of this distinct sectarian culture is cross-cut by external forces. The structure of workplace relations, for example, links the Protestant working class to wider economic institutions. Sectarianism is not the only important social relationship which concerns Protestant workers. Before the outbreak of the current phase of the conflict, the Northern Irish State had been widely perceived as resting upon an essentially paternalistic relationship between the Unionist bourgeoisie and the PWC.[11] The PWC belief that its livelihood rested upon its support for the Stormont Government, the Unionist Party and the Orange Order was encouraged by the middle- and upper-class leadership of those institutions. One Loyalist paramilitary member summarises the essential character of the relationship:

Coal lorries bedecked with Union Jacks and carrying flute bands appeared as if by magic. Unionist candidates (they were always Orangemen) would appeal to the working-class electorate with impassioned pleas. They always resurrected the border along with the Orange card, and our people would turn up and vote *en masse* for an Orangeman. These same candidates would then disappear for another four years, leaving us in the belief that Catholics were 'second-class citizens' and we had more going for us as Protestants.[12]

Such a relationship was never likely to encourage ideas of self-help from within the PWC. The view popularised in recent years of the PWC as socially content, based upon a recognition of their status within the unionist bloc, must be questioned. As Bew et al.[13] have identified, there has been almost-continuous conflict within unionism, surrounding the tensions between the populist and anti-populist traditions.

The Ulster Defence Association: origins and growth

It was within this environment that the UDA emerged. Its most embryonic form, the Shankill Defence Association, was actually formed to oppose the effects the Belfast Urban Renewal Programme was having on the local area. This, however, coincided with a worsening security situation. In response the group, 'readily turned into a paramilitary group patrolling the upper Shankill and the border with the Catholic Falls'. However, 'its social aims were never neglected'.[14] Loyalist Defence Organisations were formed throughout Northern Ireland but mainly in urban centres, especially Belfast. Originally there was little co-ordination, and 'vigilante' groups were responsible for the erection of barricades and for the protection of individual or small clusters of streets. As the Provisional Irish Republican Army emerged from the split in the republican movement, and Catholic opposition to internment intensified, the loyalist vigilante organisations began to take a more permanent form. The UDA central organisation grew in importance as local groups began to amalgamate and organise. By 1972 the UDA had around 40,000 members and parades, featuring mass-ranked members wearing military uniform, became commonplace.[15]

This development seemed legitimate to many working-class loyalists given their social construction of the world. The following statement captures their overall feeling well:

Uncertainty aroused great fear among Protestants that their presumed millennium of Stormont solidarity, secured by whatever the government of the day might impose under the Special Powers Act under the protection of Westminster statute – and the convention of Westminster blind eyes – was suddenly vulnerable.[16]

In the early days of the UDA the leadership was composed of prominent members of the local community. Those immediately in charge tended to be 'shrewd street leaders – local bookies, garage hands or small businessmen'.[17] The dominance of this faction gave the UDA its initial direction and momentum. Their demands were clearly reflected in the general demands to 'wage war on the IRA', and that 'Stormont must rule'.

No doubt many who joined the UDA and fully supported such aims saw themselves as defending the sectarian base of the State and were prepared to do so by military means. However, from its inception the UDA contained a number of different ideological positions. The organisation's history reveals almost continuous factional disputes. Some of this merely reflects the organisation's involvement in 'protection' and the setting-up and management of 'drinking clubs'. But it also reflects the fact that as an organisation with a mass base it contained a criminal element. Other disputes involved individuals and 'power-struggles' aimed at demarcating control in localised areas. Serious disagreements have also arisen from differences over the direction of both military and ideological struggles.

An early example of this was the UDA's relationship with the Ulster Vanguard Movement, led by ex-official Unionist politician, William Craig. The Vanguard Movement articulated the sense of 'betrayal' by Britain that many unionists were feeling. In doing so it earned considerable working-class support. Craig's main aim was to reconstruct the old unionist alliance in order to protect what remained of indigenous capital and the Protestant ascendancy.[18] It was also the Vanguard which first mooted the idea of independence. In a series of newspaper advertisements during 1973, Vanguard sought to present a Unilateral Declaration of Independence as a real alternative to union with Britain. In one pamphlet it declared:

> We shall assert our right to take whatsoever action we consider necessary to safeguard our Loyalist cause . . . such action to include, if there is no alternative, the establishment of an Independent British Ulster.[19]

The Vanguard notion of independence should not be regarded as a precursor of more recent demands for withdrawal from the United Kingdom. As we shall see, subsequent calls for an

Independent Ulster from Loyalist paramilitaries mark a break from, rather than a continuation of, Vanguard's attempt to reconstruct the old unionist alliance within an independent structure. As early as 1972 there were growing voices of dissension within paramilitary ranks from those who were becoming increasingly articulate in their criticisms of middle-class unionist politicians – as the following statement from the then Chairperson, James Anderson, shows:

> I feel that people are beginning to catch on about the Unionist government. The ordinary man is starting to think for himself about the fifty years of misrule that we did have. If a Unionist candidate came down a street, all he had to do was wave a flag and beat a drum and he was elected for the next five years, and you didn't see him for the next five years. People are starting to catch on.[20]

Tensions became overt when a section of the UDA issued a press statement in which it was claimed that 'class-conscious elements' were forming a new body called the 'Ulster Citizens Army', and expressed concern that ex-unionist politicians were becoming too influential in UDA planning. The statement continued, 'These parasites, who never in the past were the friend of the Ulster worker, have not changed. Their sole aim is still the pursuit of power at any price.'[21] Such unease could not have been relieved by the following statement from the leader of the Loyalist Association of Workers (LAW), the largest of the Loyalist workplace organisations:

> The children of the workers deserve the opportunity of higher education, and . . . they are not getting it here today. Where there ought to be rows of terraced houses with modern bathrooms, up-to-date playing fields and old people's homes, swimming pools and normal necessities of life today, the Shankill Road and other workers' areas present a bleak picture of desolation. . . . The leaders of unionism have not inherited our automatic support.[22]

Reaction to this developing 'class-conscious' line of argument was rapid, dramatic and bloody. In an intense campaign within the UDA, those in any way associated with this radical line were assassinated or forced to flee the country.[23] The more 'military'-orientated members of the UDA took control. As a result the number of sectarian murders rose dramatically. It was pointed out at the time that, 'the greater part of the near 200 such assassinations were committed by Protestants organised in groups for this specific purpose.'[24]

The UDA, however, was being forced to adopt a number of conflicting roles. For example it increasingly found itself in a position of direct confrontation with the British Army, especially after it adopted a strategy of setting-up 'no-go' areas,[25] in protest at the continuation of such areas in republican districts. In May 1972 there was rioting in East Belfast after members of the parachute regiment demolished loyalist barricades. While in July, following the establishment of 'permanent' loyalist 'no-go' areas in Belfast, around 10,000 UDA members confronted the British Army in the north of the city in the most serious incident to date. Such confrontations marked important perceptual changes within the PWC. The accusations of British army brutality, for long a refrain from the Catholic community, could no longer be dismissed as 'Republican propaganda'. Furthermore, a growing number of Loyalists were being detained under the Special Powers Act.

The Ulster Workers' Council strike, 1974

Such considerations were, however, rapidly shelved in the light of the Ulster Workers' Council (UWC) strike in May 1974. The UWC had emerged as an amalgamation of loyal workplace organisations. The events surrounding the 'strike' have been well documented.[26] Briefly, the strike began on Wednesday 15 May, following the ratification of the Sunningdale Agreement by the Northern Irish Assembly. Initially there was much confusion, but, as the strike progressed, the UWC, supported on the streets by loyalist paramilitaries, took control of the distribution of electricity, and gas and petrol supplies. As the strike gained momentum the UWC regulated the opening of retail shops, places of entertainment and the rationing of petrol. Hundreds of thousands were on strike or unable to attend work. One commentator summarised the situation as follows: 'The UWC controlled everything – milk, bread, petrol and even passes for essential workers, like doctors, to get around.'[27]

The turning point in favour of the UWC appeared to be when Harold Wilson, the British Prime Minister, made a speech on the national media, in which he declared that 'the people of Ulster spent their lives sponging on Westminster'. During the following days many people in Belfast wore sponges in their lapels in protest. At best the speech was counter-productive in its influence on loyalist opinion. As the strike reached its second week, the UWC shut-down Belfast's gas supply and began to run down to a crisis point the electricity supply for the whole of Northern Ireland. On Tuesday 28 May the Northern Ireland Executive collapsed and the strike ended the next day.

Unionist hegemony did reconstruct itself, as it is always likely to do when a threat is perceived to the constitutional position. (It did so again, for example, in the initial phase of resistance to the Anglo-Irish agreement in 1985.) But, once this immediate fear is overcome, class tensions are always likely to resurface. As Fisk pointed out, when the strike ended in 1974, 'the politicians and paramilitary leaders retreated to their old position of mutual distrust.'[28]

The strike had far-reaching consequences for relations within the unionist bloc. The widespread involvement of the PWC in community action during the strike in fact marked a distinct break with the corporate ideology of Orangeism. It is important to note that the paramilitary groups, and the subsequent community groups, developed from the same base. Often they relied upon the same people and drew upon the same physical structure. The experience of the strike led some within the PWC to question their own structural position. This emergent consciousness is reflected in this statement from a paramilitary spokesperson some ten years later:

> The Loyalist community has been brainwashed for years. We are supposed to be the privileged class yet we live in atrocious conditions, houses with no baths, run-down estates, high unemployment, few social amenities and whole communities which are dying because of the planners and government policies. Yet for years people have continued to vote for politicians who created and allowed these conditions to exist. People vote out of fear.[29]

The UDA was forced to reconsider its position fundamentally. Under pressure from the PWC it sought to respond in a way which ensured that the momentum of the strike was not lost. Initially it tried to establish a joint working committee with leading loyalist politicians. The latter, however, rejected this suggestion and remained intensely suspicious of any level of independent action by the PWC. One consequence of this was that the UDA seemed to lose its sense of direction, giving rise to a legitimation crisis concerning its role within loyalist areas. Increasingly accusations of 'gangsterism' were heard in traditional working-class areas such as inner East Belfast, especially as the perceived threat from neighbouring Catholic districts had receded. In addition, throughout 1975, the UDA and UVF were engaged in a bloody feud resulting in the killing of several members of each organisation. Furthermore, those who had joined the organisation to 'fight for Ulster' simply were not interested in, or capable of, fulfilling the role of community workers.[30] The growing alienation from the wider PWC community was heightened in 1977 when the UDA gave its support to an indefinite strike called by the Rev. Ian Paisley in an attempt to force the government to implement stronger security measures. On the first day of the 'strike' many workplaces remained open and the police, unlike 1974, responded to incidents of intimidation and removed barricades. Most notably throughout the strike power-station workers failed to give their support. The strike was an abject failure made worse by the obvious comparison with the UWC strike.

At the time the segmentation of the unionist bloc was increasing and manifested itself in open hostility between the UDA and the Democratic Unionist Party. In the face of a weakening position and a growing crisis of legitimation the leadership of the UDA resolved its immediate problem by conceding ground to members who were calling for a coherent social and political programme. However, the consequences of the 1977 strike for the UDA were profound and far-reaching. Andy Tyrie who lead the organisation until quite recently expressed the position as follows:

> The British Government stopped taking the Loyalist community seriously after 1977 because they saw them so divided . . . the most it [the British Government] can expect from most Loyalists is to march about and protest. But if it means taking on the British establishment in a civil-war situation, that is totally different.[31]

New political directions?

The most immediate political outcome was the formation of the New Ulster Political Research Group (NUPRG) to promote the idea of an 'Independent Ulster' as the solution to the problems of

Northern Ireland. Simultaneously the UDA made a conscious effort to strengthen its position at the community level by way of the Ulster Community Action Group (UCAG). The following statement from the NUPRG's Chairperson captured the mood of the UDA's thinking:

> The problem to date has been that the UDA has always relied on the established politicians to represent them politically. But we believe that over the last few years that representation hasn't been reflecting the true feelings of grass-root people.

He went on to outline the reasons for such disillusionment:

> On the Loyalist side the Loyalist politicians have manipulated the Protestant people . . . on the Catholic side they have been used and manipulated by emotional-type politicians. Because over the years if you look at politics in Northern Ireland no one has talked about pure politics. Every election time, all you have is a flag being waved at you repeating threats to your constitutional position.[32]

The major intellectual output of the NUPRG was a discussion document, *Beyond the Religious Divide*, first published in March 1979. It contained a series of proposals for the introduction of an 'Independent Ulster'. The basis of this was to be a constitution based on the American Presidential system, and a 'Bill of Rights'. It is worth quoting at length the Editorial of *Ulster*, the weekly magazine of the UDA at the time:

> Unionist politics have dominated Ulster because of the absence of a strong labour movement. This absence allows Britain to keep a policy of conditional support for the union while at the same time continuing to explore ways and means of uniting Ireland in cooperation with the Dublin Government. This is fertile ground for sectarian politics.
>
> The Ulster Defence Association came into being as an expression of the mistrust of Ulster working people with Unionist politics. The UDA is a working people's organisation, the only one of its kind in Ulster. While its main concern has been for the maintenance of an armed body of citizens, the UDA has found itself in the position of exploring

its political potential, because of the increasingly obvious weakness of Unionist politics.[33]

Under this momentum the UDA entered the field of constitutional politics. The Ulster Loyalist Democratic Party (ULDP) was formed. Hopes of a breakthrough into the party-political arena proved disappointing. The main spokesperson of the ULDP, John McMichael, stood in a by-election in South Belfast but polled only 1.3 per cent of the vote. The ULDP again fielded candidates in the 1985 local elections with equally disastrous results. The nationalist population understandably saw the initiative as a proposal to bring back a loyalist-dominated state. Among the PWC, support was minimal and this is even true of UDA members. The ability of the UDA to permeate PWC consciousness as a whole seems weak. The UDA spokesperson in discussing the idea of an independent Ulster had this to say concerning the lack of electoral support: 'Protestants see independence as a stepping stone to a United Ireland. There's a fear that if you break the link with the UK you leave yourself wide open.'[34]

'Ulster' culture and identity

Increasingly the UDA has sought to promote their notion of an independent Ulster on the idea of a 'shared identity'. This involves an historical reconstruction and is based largely on the works of Adamson.[35] These seek to show that the origins of the Protestant population in the north of Ireland predate the sixteenth-century Plantation of Ulster. Adamson argues that the 'Cruthin', the original inhabitants of Ireland, were driven north by invading Gaels and their last foothold in Ireland was in what is now Antrim and Down. Many, however, fled to Scotland, strengthening the historical link between the Scottish and Irish populations. The Plantation then can be seen as a 'homecoming'.

This interpretation of history has been associated with the adoption of a number of symbols and hero figures from Irish history and pre-history which previously had been seen as the property of Irish Republicanism. Of particular importance are the events of the Tain Bo Cuailnge which forms the centre-piece of the eighth-century Ulster cycle of heroic tales. It concerns the invasion of Ulster by the forces of the King and Queen of Connaught. The hero of the tale is Cuchullain, the Hound of Ulster, who resists the armies single-handed. The adoption of

Cuchullain as a popular image by the UDA is particularly significant as it was previously used only in republican imagery. For example, a commemorative statue of Cuchullain erected to the 1916 rebels stands in the GPO in Dublin, and it has also featured in medals issued by the Army of the Republic of Ireland. Adamson sees this as a total misrepresentation of history and outlines what he sees as the consequence for contemporary politics:

> So total has become the Gaelic domination in language and culture that even in these modern times Gaelic Ireland is synonomous with Irish Nationalism, and the Gaelic tongue is unequivocally known as Irish. That the Irish Gaels suffered under late English domination is but one side of the coin which carries on its reverse the long cruel extermination of the population and culture of the ancient kindred of the Ulster people.[36]

This reading of Irish history is, of course, highly questionable and controversial and I would not attempt to demonstrate its accuracy. But this is not important. What is of importance is the effect it has had on UDA thinking and strategy and the consciousness of the PWC. The popularity of Adamson's original works has resulted in a growing body of literature within loyalism.[37] It has also produced a continuing debate within the UDA on questions concerned with identity and history. That such a debate is necessary is attested by the words of a UDA spokesperson:

> The more we talked to people and asked 'what's it all about?' the more we got the same answers, 'no surrender', 'remember 1690', 'fuck the Pope'. . . . We did a survey asking people when Protestants came to Ulster. When was the Plantation? and a lot of other things. A lot of people thought we came here just before World War One, because the only thing they knew was that their Grandfathers were in the war, at the Somme . . . nothing before that, absolutely nothing.[38]

Another spokesperson pointed out that:

> Historically, Ulster people, if they got interested at all, drifted into British Empire culture; Opera, Ballet and Theatre . . . we hoped to interest people in something beside pop

groups and TV . . . we wanted to get back to a sense of our own community.[39]

The resulting search for identity has led to some strange developments. The UDA now has an official poet who contributes regularly to the Ulster magazine. Its last supreme commander Andy Tyrie has co-written a play, 'This Is It', the central notion of which is Protestant working-class culture. In it, one of the central characters, Sam, claims:

We're so paranoid about anything that seems 'Fenian' or 'Irish'. . . . You talk to an Ulster Prod about traditional music or dancing and he'll think you a 'Fenian-lover'. The bloody Prods have denied half their own history . . .[40]

Such ideas have, of course, not gone unchallenged within Unionism. Apart from objections from traditional unionist circles, a counter-literature has also appeared. This concedes the notion of a distinct 'Ulster' identity, but defines it as an 'Ulster-British culture and heritage' (Ulster Society 1986). This closely resembles the literature produced by the Ulster Vanguard movement in the early 1970s rather than that currently being produced by the UDA.

It is important then to try to assess how far the UDA's thinking has permeated PWC consciousness. In an attitude survey conducted in 1967, before the outbreak of the current phase of the conflict, 32 per cent of Protestants chose 'Ulster', as their national identity.[41] Ten years later another major survey shows that those chosing 'Ulster' as their first option had fallen to around 20 per cent.[42] There are, however, considerable variations within the unionist bloc by socio-economic status, and there is significant working-class support for some form of Independent Northern Ireland. Of equal importance is the high percentage of the PWC who chose 'Ulster' as their second choice. It is this group who would choose independence in a situation where Britain declared an intention to withdraw.[43]

Contemporary loyalist popular culture

One example of the effect of these attitudes on the wider loyalist cultural tradition can be seen by examining working-class loyalist literature. Since 1969, a number of poems, pieces of prose and songs extolling the heroic and martial aspects of loyalist working-class life have appeared. One early example of this type of loyalist literature, which is both overtly sectarian and supportive of violence, is the following lyric, entitled 'Dear Sniper':

> You must feel good, now don't you?
> A virile rat and strong
> Like others of your witches' brew
> Who use the gun and bomb
>
> But here's a little food for thought
> That you might contemplate
> Some Vermin run before they're caught
> But Orange Tom Cats fear for nought
> And Rats exterminate[44]

A contemporary song, in the same vein, explicitly praises the military virtues of the UDA:

> This song is near and dear to me
> A song of truth and liberty
> Of the boys who'll beat the IRA
> Those loyal men of the UDA
>
> [Chorus]:
>
> For 30,000 men have we
> Who'll fight to keep our Ulster free
> We're on our guard, both night and day
> For we're the men of the UDA
>
> Those Rebel scum can't bear the light
> They kill and murder in the night
> But time draws near to their domesday
> They'll be destroyed by the UDA
>
> Now this advice I'll freely give
> To all those Rebels who wish to live
> Lay down your arms this very day
> You cannot beat the UDA
>
> So lift your glass and toast away
> To the UDA and victory
> For they will surely win the day
> So here's good luck to the UDA.[45]

Some of these songs have now been in existence since the early 1970s but have changed over the last 20 years. One early and extremely popular example was the following song, sung to the tune of the 'Red River Valley':

Have you heard of the Battle of the Shankhill
Where most of the fighting was done
It was there that a young UVF man
Was shot by an IRA gun

As he lay on the battlefield dying
With the blood running out of his head
He turned to the bastards that shot him
And these are the words that he said

God bless my wife in the dear old Shankhill
God bless my home and family too
God bless the flag that I fight under
The Union Jack, Red, White and Blue[46]

Significantly in the contemporary version the final verse has changed to:

Will you bury me under the Red Hand
Will you bury me in Ulster's clay
Will you bury me under the Red Hand
For my fighting for Ulster is done.[47]

There are many other songs popular in Loyalist pubs and clubs throughout Belfast which demonstrate an allegiance to an 'Ulster' identity, or at least a duality of national consciousness which is not explicitly 'British'. Consider the words of this song:

The Red Hand's my emblem
The Sash is my song
To the Republic of Ireland
We'll never belong
We have only six counties
But we're proud and true
And we'll always be loyal to that Red Hand so true.

And the Red White and Blue boys
That part of our cause
It gave us our freedom religion and laws

We'll fight to defend it
With heart and with hand
And we'll never be driven from this Ulster land.[48]

The majority of such pieces, of course, retain overtly sectarian messages. However, in recent years there has been a parallel literature from within loyalism which suggests a different set of attitudes:

To see a baby blown to bits
Is not a pleasant thing
To be the cause of that is worse by far
To say it was for 'Ulster' or for 'Ireland'
Come to that
Is much akin to wishing on a star

We have no right to execute
Or silence or condemn
Those people unconnected to the fight
To kill and maim, assassinate
For one cause or another
Polarises us
And thats not right.[49]

This partly reflects the claim of the UDA leadership to have moved away from sectarian attacks towards what they identify as 'Republican activists'.

For some the notion of an 'Ulster identity' is simply to be used as a weapon in a continuing propaganda war. The following statement summarises this position well:

The political relevance of culture today can be clearly seen when one examines the way our enemies especially in Sinn Fein have hijacked the so-called 'Gaelic culture' of Ireland. They have made street names and schools into political issues which they exploit and by reason of the fact they we reject this so-called Irish culture, they claim that we are not Irishmen; and therefore have no right to claim this Country as our own.[50]

Others, however, continue to use the notion of an 'Ulster identity' as a platform for political expression. The latest political development from the UDA comes in the form of another

discussion document, *Common Sense*. It is a blueprint for devolved government, 'power-sharing', with a written constitution, requiring a two-thirds majority for change. Part of the
document argues:

> There is no section of this divided Ulster community which is
> totally innocent or indeed totally guilty, totally right or
> wrong. We all share the responsibility for creating the
> situation, either by deed or by acquiescence. Therefore we
> must share the responsibility for finding a settlement and
> then share the responsibility of maintaining good govern-
> ment.[51]

According to the UDA this would allow politicians to be released
from '"the treadmill of border politics" and tackle the real
enemies of social deprivation, economic recession, unemployment and housing.'[52]

The UDA and unionist politicians

Another consistent feature of UDA thinking has been hostility
towards established unionist politicians. Two groupings, which
have had a profound effect on UDA ideology in this respect, are
loyalist paramilitary support organisations and loyalist ex-
prisoner associations. Throughout the 1980s the UDA have been
disillusioned by the lack of support given to them by unionist
politicians during several campaigns surrounding the conditions
of loyalist prisoners. As one member active in Loyalist Prisoners'
Aid explained:

> ninety-five per cent of the people I know would never have
> seen the inside of a prison if it wasn't for the present
> situation. The reason why they're in there is the Martin
> Smyths and the Bill Craigs and the Paisleys. Now if you
> listen to them, Paisley's still shouting about civil war . . . still
> wants to use the muscles of the paramilitaries if it suits him.[53]

The loyalist ex-prisoners' association has continued to warn of
the dangers of manipulation by the Unionist leadership claiming
they have repeatedly plunged the community into turmoil 'by
their cul-de-sac politics'.[54] Other UDA members are hostile
towards the Unionist leadership in general, and Ian Paisley in

particular, because of their lack of political leadership. The following statement captures this feeling well:

> It can be safely said that in the last ten years not one constructive idea has emerged out of Paisley's head. Indeed his 'political tactics' and 'know-how' amount to little more than huffing and puffing . . . a Paisley has never actually led our people anywhere but has merely voiced and reflected their fears and opinions. He is merely the politics of reaction, coupled with the blood-thirsty threats of things to come should the English even betray Ulster to Eire.[55]

This view illustrates the uneasy alliance between the UDA and Unionist politicians. In the period immediately following the signing of the Anglo-Irish agreement the leadership of the UDA gave their full support to the leaders of the UUP and DUP. Thus when a Day of Action was called on 3 March 1986 UDA members were actively involved in the 'setting-up of hundreds of road-blocks across the province to ensure it was effective'.[56] The day ended in widespread rioting in loyalist areas and snipers firing on the Royal Ulster Constabulary. As a result Unionist party leaders excluded the UDA from further mass protests. In consequence the anniversary rally against the Agreement in November 1986 and the 'Day of Defiance' in April 1987 were extremely badly supported. The UDA called for the resignation of both Paisley and Molyneaux, claiming that 'the grassroots are totally dis-affected by the lack of direction, it is no use saying No, No, No . . . Ian Paisley keeps isolating sections of the loyalist com-munity, he only wants to work with so-called "respectable people".'[57]

The relationship between the UDA and Unionist politicians is not the direct one it is sometimes assumed to be. One leading member expressed this forcibly when he said:

> Are we just tin soldiers, robots that somebody blows a whistle and we make the right noises, programmed to react and we all come marching out of the box and kick all round us . . . and when they [Unionist Politicians] think its OK – that they've made their point – with the British Government, or the Catholics, or the Southern Government, that they blew their whistles and we all neatly march back into our box . . . the trouble is that every time we come out less and less of us went back in.[58]

Community politics and the UDA

The UDA have also continued to develop strong networks of informal social welfare. For the first time in many years, recent copies of *Ulster* have carried advertisements appealing for voluntary workers to join the Ulster Community Action Group. In Belfast there are four permanent UDA 'advice centres' which are mainly concerned with issues important in day-to-day life in working-class areas: housing, DHSS enquiries and grants. They also provide, through the Loyalist Prisoners' Association, a wide range of support functions for the families of loyalist paramilitary members in prison. These range from simple financial support, to transport for prison visits, and the provision of parcels and daily newspapers to prisoners. In recent years they have provided summer holidays for the children of prisoners. A recent view of the role of community politics from *Ulster* is worth mentioning:

> Some people have told us that as a community group we should 'keep out of politics'. But one of our aims as a community group is to widen the debate from mere constitutional issues to more pressing social issues which many Protestants and Catholics face. Many of those, including our politicians, who have tried to stifle the political debate, who have tried to claim groups such as ours are 'disloyal' are the same ones who stand by ignoring the needs of the people . . . politics concerns every aspect of our lives – our personal relationships, the electric bill, power structures, the papers we read, the education we receive and who we receive it with, the dampness in the house – all deeply political. Community issues are not the preserve of 'commies' or 'rebels', and politics are not the preserve of politicians.[59]

Military reorganisation

Such views differ radically from those being projected by the UDA in the early 1970s. There have, however, also been significant structural changes in the military organisation of the UDA. Concerned initially with growing political support for Sinn Fein and, more recently, with the Anglo-Irish agreement, there has been increased pressure for the UDA to adopt a more military role. These feelings have been articulated by several leading members of the inner council. A spokesperson explained the development in the following way:

> First of all we think that there's greater and greater polaris- ation between the two communities. The turning point was really the 1981 Republican hunger strike. Since then there's been a growing polarisation and we don't see anything that's likely in the foreseeable future to close the gap.[60]

The UDA initially concluded that 'the Loyalist people want a Loyalist army beyond what they see as established controlled groups'. The Ulster Defence Force (UDF) came into existence as a 'reserve army' to be used in a 'domesday situation':

> the Loyalist paramilitaries have realised the need for a tough, well trained and disciplined army to defend Ulster . . . We have been used by politicians for too long. We are regroup- ing and reorganising.[61]

However, little has been heard of the UDF since its formation. The UDA's current military campaign against republicans has been carried out by Ulster Freedom Fighters (UFF). The UFF is now widely recognised as a 'nom de guerre' for a group within the UDA. This overall structure broadly follows the outline decided during the reorganisation of the UDA in 1983, which marked a more formal separation of the political and military roles. It has been suggested that the organisation was restruc- tured into two major components. Firstly, 'Promotion', which can be sub-divided into 'Education', 'Politics' and 'Public Re- lations', and secondly 'Protection', which revolves mainly around the activities of the UDF, and the UFF.[62] The reason for this was not simply an attempt to increase formal bureaucracy. It was, rather, an attempt by the UDA Council to come to terms with various factions within the organisation. The existence of internal divisions within the UDA has been clearly shown in recent times. John McMichael, the leading figure within the UDLP and inner-council member of the UDA, was killed on 22 December 1987 by the Provisional IRA. There followed a series of disputes within the organisation surrounding allegations of corruption and racketeering. As factional divisions became overt, the UDA's Supreme Commander, Andy Tyrie, was forced to resign, in March 1988, after a vote of no confidence by the majority of his brigade commanders. The new leadership has

promised to 'clear out the racketeers' from within the organisation. Meanwhile there have been severe recriminations within
the organisation following claims that McMichael had been set-up
by people inside the UDA.[63]

The current joint leadership of brigade commanders has not
indicated any major ideological change. The 'political' direction of
the UDA is still given by the 'McMichael principles'. Eight ULDP
candidates stood in the 1989 local council elections on a manifesto
based on the 'commonsense' document. They were successful in
having a councillor elected to Londonderry City Council. There
has, however, been a distinct change in emphasis within the UDA.
A cursory glance at the *Ulster* magazine reveals a move towards
promoting military activities,[64] and a declaration that it will step up
attacks on 'Republican activists'.[65] Although the new leadership
has claimed 'ordinary Catholics have nothing to fear' (*Guardian*, 17
March 1988), in the past the distinction between the two has not
always been clear, especially to 'ordinary Catholics'.

Towards an explanation

How is the UDA's development best explained? According to
several writers, the UDA's role is clear. It operates simply as the
military wing of the loyalist state.[66] Such an analysis reveals a
profoundly one-sided view of unionist politics. It also implies that
class relationships within unionism are static, and that hegemony
is fixed and total. In analysing the role of the UDA, sectarianism is
an important feature. It is not, however, the only element, nor is it
all-encompassing. To dismiss the UDA in terms of a manifestation
of 'mindless sectarianism' is to deny the nature of the organisation,
a broad-based coalition, often pulling in contradictory directions.
In the short term, especially following McMichael's death, those
promoting a military war to 'terrorise the terrorists' have the upper
hand. McMichael is far from unique, however, within the history
of loyalist paramilitaries, and it is possible that a grouping
consisting of more progressive elements may re-emerge. What is
clear is that PWC culture and UDA politics are far from
uni-dimensional. The position of the PWC is far from settled, and
any serious analyst should resist premature closure of the debate.
As one ex-member of the UDA put it, before there can be any full
understanding of the conflict, it is necessary

> to accept such paramilitary existence as part of community
> culture, and not something which can be conveniently

isolated or ignored. It is a grave mistake to simply and totally equate the word 'violence' as the main yardstick when explaining paramilitary existence. There must be a clear understanding of why our community bred the need for paramilitarism in the first place.[67]

References

1. H. Griffiths, 'Community Reaction and Voluntary Involvement', in J. Darby and A. Williamson, eds., *Violence and the Social Services in Northern Ireland* (Heinemann, 1978), pp. 165–200.
2. See D. Boulton, *The UVF* (Torc, 1973); S. Nelson, *Ulster's Uncertain Defenders* (Appletree, 1984).
3. *Ulster*, March 1989, p. 3.
4. *Ulster*, April 1989, p. 2.
5. R. Harbinson, *No Surrender* (Faber and Faber, 1960), pp. 131–132.
6. J. Boyd, *Out of My Class* (Blackstaff, 1985), p. 176.
7. See for example, F. Burton, *The Politics of Legitimacy* (Routledge and Kegan Paul, 1978); D. P. Barnett and A. Booth, *Orange and Green* (Northern Friends Peace Board, 1972); J. Hickie and R. S. P. Elliott, *Ulster: A Case Study in Conflict Theory* (Longman, 1971).
8. R. Rose, *Governing Without Consensus* (Faber and Faber, 1971), p. 75.
9. R. Weiner, *The Rape and Plunder of the Shankill* (Farset, 1978), p. 76.
10. See D. Hammond, *Steel Chest: The Belfast Shipyard, a Story of the People by the People* (Flying Fox, 1986) and R. Weiner, note 9, pp. 70–71 for excellent outlines of the social structure of traditional Protestant working-class communities in Belfast. The structure of such communities has no doubt been romanticised: other everyday events in traditional working-class communities such as wife beating, family disputes and other types of dependency, should also be mentioned.
11. See B. Probert, *Beyond Orange and Green* (Zed Press, 1978), pp. 48–56, and Griffith, note 1, pp. 165–168.
12. S. Sloan, cited in *Fortnight*, No. 185, p. 18.
13. See P. Bew, P. Gibbon and H. Patterson, *The State in Northern Ireland* (MUP, 1979); P. Bew and H. Patterson, *The British State and the Ulster Crisis* (Verso, 1985); P. Bew, P. Gibbon and H. Patterson, 'Some Aspects of Nationalism and Socialism in Ireland 1968–1978', in A. Morgan and B. Purdie, eds., *Ireland: Divided Nation, Divided Class* (Ink Links, 1980).
14. P. Buckland, *A History of Northern Ireland* (Gill and Macmillan, 1981), p. 128.
15. Estimates of UDA strength at this time vary considerably, from 20,000 to 60,000. However, in what must be regarded as a fairly reliable source, Flackes suggests the UDA had 40,000 members.

W.D. Flackes, *Northern Ireland: A Political Directory* (BBC, 1983), p. 229.

16. C. McKeown, *The Passion of Peace* (Blackstaff, 1984), p. 44.
17. R. Fisk, *The Point of No Return: The Strike Which Broke the British in Ulster* (Andre Deutsch, 1975), p. 28.
18. B. Probert, note 11, pp. 117–24.
19. Ulster Vanguard Movement, *Ulster – a Nation* (Vanguard, 1972), p. 10.
20. *Belfast Telegraph*, 19 September 1972.
21. Cited in Boulton, note 2, p. 178.
22. Cited in T. W. Moody, *The Ulster Question 1603–1973* (Mercier, 1974), p. 64.
23. See M. Dillon and D. Lehane, *Political Murder in Northern Ireland* (Penguin, 1973), pp. 148–49. This book provides a very useful overview of the tensions within loyalist paramilitary groups at this time. See also Boulton, note 2, and Probert, note 11.
24. Dillon and Lehane, note 23, p. 24.
25. D. Hamill, *Pig in the Middle, The Army in Northern Ireland* (Methuen, 1985), p. 129.
26. The day-to-day detail of the strike has been recorded in admirable detail by R. Fisk, note 17. See also Nelson, note 2, pp. 155–69; Buckland, note 14, pp. 169–173; Hamill, note 25, pp. 144–154.
27. Hamill, note 25, p. 147.
28. Fisk, note 17, p. 28.
29. *Shankill Bulletin*, September 1984, p. 5.
30. See Nelson, note 2, pp. 193–202.
31. *Fortnight*, No. 204, p. 5.
32. Cited in J. Holland, *Too Long a Sacrifice* (Penguin, 1982), pp. 112–113.
33. *Ulster*, Vol. 2, No. 3, 1978.
34. Interview, UDA HQ, May 1985.
35. See I. Adamson, *The Cruthin* (Donard, 1974) and *The Identity of Ulster* (Donard, 1982).
36. Adamson, *The Cruthin*, p. 15.
37. See for example Ulster Young Unionist Council, *Cuchuliann – The Lost Legend* (UYUC, 1986).
38. Interview, UDA HQ, May 1985.
39. A. Tyrie, cited in *Belfast Review*, 10 (May 1985), p. 2.
40. The play was printed in full in *Theatre Ireland*, No. 7, 1982, pp. 19–34.
41. See Rose, note 8, p. 485.
42. See E. Moxon Brown, *Nation, Class and Creed in Northern Ireland* (Gower, 1983), p. 6.
43. See J. W. McAuley, 'Will Ulster Fight?', *New Society*, July 1987.
44. Cited in B. Rolson, *Escaping from Belfast*.
45. I recorded this and the subsequent songs in various loyalist pubs and clubs in Belfast during fieldwork trips between 1985 and 1987.
46. For a slightly different version see R. Jenkins, *Hightown Rules:*

Growing Up in a Belfast Housing Estate (NYB, 1982), p. 37.
47. See note 45.
48. As above.
49. S. Duddy, *Concrete Whirlpools of the Mind* (Ulidia Press, 1983), p. 17.
50. Ulster Young Unionist Council, note 37, p. 2.
51. 'Commonsense: Northern Ireland – an Agreed Process' (The Ulster Political Research Group, no date), p. 2. [Published 1987].
52. Cited in *Belfast Telegraph*, 29 January 1987.
53. Interview, UDA HQ, June 1986.
54. Cited in *The Sunday News*, 1 February 1987.
55. *Ulster*, May 1987, pp. 4–5.
56. A. Glueke, *Northern Ireland: The International Perspective* (Gill and Macmillan, 1988), p. 76.
57. Cited in *The Shankill Bulletin*, Easter 1987, p. 1.
58. Interview, UDA HQ, June 1986.
59. *Ulster*, December 1985, p. 2.
60. Interview, UDA HQ, May 1985.
61. Ulster, April 1985, p. 9.
62. See A. Aughrey and D. Hume, 'Developments Within the UDA: A New Paramilitary Emphasis', *Teaching Politics*, Vol. 15, Pt. 2 (May 1978), pp. 315–327.
63. See for example, *Ulster*, November 1988, pp. 12–14.
64. There is now considerable evidence to suggest that loyalist paramilitary groups have acquired considerable stockpiles of arms since 1985. On 15 May 1989 the UVF deployed an RGP-7 rocket launcher against a Sinn Fein advice centre. The UDA now also appear better armed than ever before. See *Fortnight*, No. 273, p. 11, and No. 274, p. 15.
65. See for example, *Ulster*, November 1988, December 1988, January 1989.
66. Such views are central to those who adopt an orthodox anti-imperialist analysis of the conflict. They are well represented in G. Bell, *The Protestants of Ulster* (Pluto, 1976) and *The British in Ireland* (Pluto, 1984); M. Farrell, *The Orange State* (Pluto, 1976); Irish Freedom Movement, *The Irish War* (Junis, 1985); D. Reed, *Ireland: The Key to the British Revolution* (Larkin, 1984); C. Bamber, *Ireland's Permanent Revolution* (Bookmarks, 1987).
67. Billy McKeen, 'The Roots of Peace', in *The Third Force* (Unity Press, Belfast, 19), p. 11. McKeen was a UDA member in the early 1970s. He is now a community activist, and engaged in work across the sectarian divide.

5

The Labour Party and Northern Ireland in the 1960s

Jonathan Moore

Twenty years after the arrival of troops on the streets of Ulster, the lack of political debate on Britain's role within the Six Counties remains a constant source of anger to many people in Ireland, whatever their politics. The lack of motivation within the left in Britain has been noted on many occasions. Why has the left historically felt so uncomfortable with the Irish issue? In particular there has been a question mark regarding the historic role of the Labour Party in its dealings with Ireland. Many in the party when criticising some new or alleged revisionism in party policy point to a golden age of socialist purity when Labour did not compromise or apologise for itself. Such a period has never existed in relation to Ireland. Why? This essay will deal with one short period when the party's approach to Ireland was challenged by a group of MPs and activists. The period in question was from 1964 to 1968, and the group in question was the Campaign for Democracy in Ulster (CDU). The period starts with the election of the Labour Government in 1964 and ends in October 1968 when the RUC attack a civil rights march in Derry. The latter event was televised worldwide and it forced the Labour Government to involve itself directly in Northern Irish Government affairs almost for the first time since partition. The fact that it took this bloody event to stir the British government into action is crucially important. It reflects the concerns of government both before and after 1968; always it seems that they are reacting and responding. Always as one Labour MP put it, it is a case of 'too little, too late.'[1] Why?

Joanne Karren

Labour and Ireland: the origins of policy

The return of a Labour government at Westminster in 1964, after 13 years in the political wilderness, was greeted with enthusiasm in Catholic areas of Northern Ireland. Particular faith was placed in the new Prime Minister, Harold Wilson, who was seen as sympathetic to the plight of the Catholic community in Northern Ireland. A month before taking office, Wilson had replied to a new civil rights group, The Campaign for Social Justice, in the following terms:

> I agree with you as to the importance of the issues with which your campaign is concerned and can assure you that a Labour government would do everything in its power to see that infringements of justice to which you are so rightly drawing attention are effectively dealt with.[2]

Interest in Wilson's views on the situation in Northern Ireland were further fuelled by various off-the-cuff announcements in favour of a united Ireland and by gestures such as the return of the remains of Sir Roger Casement to Ireland. Wilson's 'surrogate Irish nationalism'[3] was now going to be tested.

Wilson was not to pass this test in nationalist eyes; the reason for this had little to do with the man himself, but was grounded in the historical relationship between the Labour Party and Ireland. One book on the party and Ireland has been called *Troublesome Business*.[4] This was to prove a suitable description of Labour's attitude towards Ireland since the Party's formation earlier this century.

Concern about Ireland had played an important part in the formation of the Party. For example Hyndman from the Social Democratic Federation in 1881 claimed that 'the principal cause' of the existence of the SDF was 'the action of the Government in relation to Ireland'.[5] However, despite interest in the issue, there was also a widespread failure to differentiate Labour policy from that of the Gladstonian Liberals. Kier Hardie was typical of this, when speaking in 1892: 'Since 1879 I have been the advocate of the movement to secure Home Rule for Ireland, provided the supremacy of the Imperial Parliament be maintained unimpaired.'[6]

The party which did emerge at the turn of the century supported Home Rule in a low-profile manner. This was apparent in the Party's attitude to the 1912 Home Rule Bill. In the parliamentary party report to the 1913 conference, the objective as regards the Irish Bill was seen as being 'to get the measure carried and put out of the way'.[7] Stubbs concludes that 'By 1913 the Parliamentary Labour Party [PLP] were thoroughly frustrated with the Irish issue which was taking up an inordinate amount of time, and which was clearly blocking many necessary social reforms.'[8]

This climate of opinion was accentuated by the fact that Labour did not appear to see Ireland really as their issue. The party treated Ireland as the concern of the Liberal and Conservative parties. Ramsay Macdonald articulated this in 1914: 'We will take the position of a detached party listening to what is said, helping, as we have done during the last two years . . . Home Rule to be inscribed on the statute book of the realm.'[9]

The dramatic events of 1918 with the obliteration of constitutional nationalism in much of Ireland and its replacement by the separatist Sinn Fein did not alter basic Labour perceptions. Home Rule was still the order of the day. The 1920 Party Conference adopted the following in wonderful tones of benign imperialism:

> We believe that if Ireland were free to decide whether she would remain within the empire or become completely separated from it, the Irish themselves, upon mature consideration would decide that it was in their vital interest that the link should not be totally severed.[10]

However, despite this extraordinary refusal to accept the realities of the 1918 election, the Party was going to have to alter policy, if only because the brutality of British policy during the Irish war of independence from 1919 onwards demanded some sort of response. Under mounting pressure from certain sections of the Party, a commission of enquiry was set up to investigate Ireland.[11] Its report in 1921 signified a softening of attitude towards Sinn Fein. However, the tendency to see Ireland through the medium of British interests was seen in the commission's report, which concluded that a new Irish constituion must 'prevent Ireland from becoming a military or naval menace to Great Britain.'[12]

The logic of this was that Britain should retain some constitutional influence in Ireland. In parallel to this the Party also condemned partition as a scheme which would never 'secure the approval of the Irish people'.[13] Labour, however, did not vote against the Anglo-Irish agreement, which cemented partition and appeared happy to see the back of what Clynes, the Labour leader, called 'this troublesome subject'.[14]

The Labour Party joined the Conservatives in now leaving Northern Ireland to its own devices. Between 1921 and the 1960s the Unionists acted with great success in order to nullify the political and economic power of the Northern Nationalists. The full extent of the discrimination in virtually all walks of life was later to be documented in the Cameron Report.[15] Labour, however, did not want the thorny subject of Northern Ireland raised in the Commons. Following Speaker's rulings in 1922 and 1923, matters delegated to the regional parliament at Belfast could not be raised at Westminster.[16] Labour did not question the virtue of this convention. When Sam Kyle of the Northern Ireland Labour Party visited the British Labour Party conference in 1926, he 'did not think the people that attended the conference took any particular interest in this problem', i.e. partition.[17]

In reality a form of bi-partisanship existed between the two parties at Westminster, which was based on a desire for the Irish issue not to be reopened. There was no formal agreement between the parties, but rather an informal consensus between them to ensure that Northern Irish questions were left to Stormont. There were few critics of this within the Labour Party.

The election of the 1945 Labour government raised hopes within the nationalist communities that a wind of change could be on the horizon. However, as Rumpf and Hepburn have observed, 'It became clear at a very early stage that no-one in the Attlee cabinet was inclined to upset the Unionist applecart.'[18] However, there was a small group of Labour MPs who did wish to see the Party act. In 1946 there was formed the Friends of Ireland group within the PLP.[19] Its membership combined orthodox nationalists and reformers; all were convinced that the Labour government should intervene in the North. They intervened on various occasions to attack discrimination within the Six Counties. The response of the Labour front bench was eloquently expressed by Herbert Morrison in 1949: 'I hope that none of us will encourage . . . this Irish issue[so as to] become an embarrassing issue in British politics again.[20]

In September 1948 the Taoiseach, John A. Costello, announced that his government was leaving the Commonwealth;[21] Ireland was becoming a Republic. The British government's response was to strengthen Northern Ireland's position within the United

Kingdom through the introduction of the constitutional guarantee. Attlee told the Commons in October 1949:

> The view of His Majesty's Government of the United Kingdom has always been that no change should be made in the constitutional status of Northern Ireland without . . . [her] . . . free consent.[22]

This was later to be legally enshrined in the 1949 Ireland Bill. The Friends of Ireland organised a major revolt, but the support of the Conservative opposition ensured that it comfortably passed through the Commons.[23]

Labour thus cemented partition whilst at the same time refusing to ensure that the Catholic minority enjoyed full British rights. It was this latter problem that was to force intervention in Northern Ireland. However, it was to take violence to convince Labour that such intervention was worthwhile.

Civil rights and the rise of the CDU

The political situation in Northern Ireland from partition to the 1960s can best be understood in the context of stalemate. The Unionists ruled without outside interference; the Nationalists suffered without outside help. The latter expressed their resentment through political support for constitutional nationalism, in the form of the shambolic Nationalist party, and occasionally for the physical force tradition of the equally shambolic Republican movement. The issue of discrimination was rarely addressed by Nationalists since all problems were blamed on the border. There was little or no direct campaigning to end the discrimination. All political energy was directed towards attacking the crime of partition. However, from the early 1960s onwards, increasing sections of the Catholic community realised that this political obsession with partition was achieving nothing for the minority community. There was now a demand, particularly from within the emerging Catholic middle classes, for full participation within the Northern state. As a result of this attitudinal change, there developed civil rights organisations which focused on the widespread discrimination against the Catholic minority. The 'chimera of Irish unity'[24] was played down.

Labour MPs, particularly the new crop of 1964, were to respond to these changes in Northern Ireland. Typical of this was Paul Rose, a Manchester MP. Prior to 1962 Rose did not 'have the remotest idea about the situation'.[25] However, through contact with the Connolly Association, Rose became aware of the level of discrimination in Ulster. Importantly, from the start, his interest in Irish politics was not to do with the border, but to do 'with the rights of Northern Irish Catholics as United Kingdom citizens'.[26]

The fact that Rose and other Labour MPs stressed that the border was not an issue was to be the catalyst that was to allow Northern Ireland to become the kind of issue that mainstream Labour MPs could feel comfortable with. The topics of discrimination and civil liberties were precisely the kind of bread and butter questions that Labour MPs felt comfortable with. The Labour leadership remained quiet on the subject of civil rights in the period from 1964 to 1966. Their interest in Northern Ireland was stimulated by far less principled reasoning. In this period Labour's Commons majority was only five, and therefore the twelve Unionist MPs, all solidly Conservative, presented a real problem when the division bell rang. Wilson later recalled:

> . . . when the government had a majority of three in this house, we could have been voted down by Northern Irish members on Rachmanism in London whereas English members had no opportunity for voting on Rachmanism in Northern Ireland.[27]

The CDU wanted to turn this concern about the position of Unionist MPs into a wide-ranging discussion about Stormont–Westminster relations. Rose argued in February 1965 that 'what happens in Dungannon is as much the legitimate interest of UK MPs as what happens in Dundee or Dolgelly'.[28] However, the Labour leadership and the majority of Labour MPs were really only interested in the possibilities of 'Unionist hacks supporting the English Tory party'[29] precipitating an early general election. In late March 1965 Wilson hinted at measures limiting the voting power of Unionists in the Commons. However, the response of the Conservative leader was so forceful that the idea was instantly dropped. The result of the 1966 election, which gave Labour a large overall majority, nullified the potential Commons power of the Unionists, and so in Wilson's eyes the issue died. The episode had shown that Wilson had no interest in embroiling himself in the anomalies of Westminster–Stormont relations. However, amongst a minority of the PLP, the effect of the episode was only to increase their determination to force the government to intervene 'to uphold UK rights in Ulster'.[30] On 2

June 1965, the Campaign for Democracy in Ulster was formed. It quickly had the support of nearly 50 MPs. Rose was elected Chairman and Lord Fenner Brockway, the veteran peace campaigner, President.

The aims of this new pressure group were threefold. First, it wanted to secure a full and impartial enquiry into the administration of government in Northern Ireland and into allegations of discrimination against Catholics. Second, it wanted to examine the electoral law and in particular the vexed question of electoral boundaries. Third, the group demanded that the Race Relations Act be applied in Northern Ireland and that it be amended to include religious discrimination and incitement. What was specifically not mentioned here was any question of the border. This was clear evidence of the striking difference between the CDU and groups which had traditionally campaigned on Ireland. The very use of the word 'Ulster' in its name was a deliberate attempt to distance the organisation from being seen as a nationalist grouping. The CDU wrote in 1967:

> . . . the people of Ulster (particularly the Catholic minority) should have the same rights as the rest of the United Kingdom. The border was considered irrelevant to the issue, and the CDU relates its campaign to those parts of the United Kingdom over which the British Government had control.[31]

The call was for 'British standards' for British people. There was talk of gerrymandering but not of partition. Unionism and Republicanism alike were seen as ancient political philosophies with no utility value for the Ulster of the 1960s. The CDU wanted their cause to be akin to the civil rights movements flourishing throughout the world at this time:

> Under the able secretaryship of Paddy Byrne, Catholic, Protestant, Jew and Humanist worked together and poignantly illustrated our concern for the totality of human rights by inviting Dr. Pitt, a West Indian, to chair a delegate conference of the Labour movement in London. 'We shall overcome' was now heard in Derry and Deptford with an Irish lilt that was never expected in Alabama.[32]

The supremacy of orthodoxy; the failure of the CDU

In April 1967 representatives of the CDU visited Northern Ireland, and produced a scathing report on the state of democracy in the Six

Counties. Underlying the tactics of the CDU was a belief that the justice of their cause was so undeniable that once the Labour Government heard the facts, they would be forced to act. This was also the philosophy of Gerry Fitt, the MP for West Belfast after 1966, who, as one observer was later to write, was convinced that '. . . when Harold Wilson's Government knew the facts, they would take corrective actions in Northern Ireland'.[33] This central belief was to prove fallacious. There is no evidence that any of the senior members of the Wilson Cabinet had any desire to intervene in Northern Ireland. Rose believed that the appointment of Roy Jenkins at the Home Office meant that there was now 'a more ready ear'.[34] However, Jenkins did nothing to act on the CDU report on discrimination. The following anecdote is probably an accurate assessment of Jenkins's concerns:

> In 1967, a party of Stormont Nationalist MPs were received in Westminster by Roy Jenkins. . . . After they had presented their case, a horrified aide said to Jenkins 'something will have to be done'. Jenkins replied that nothing would be done because any Englishman who set foot in Northern Ireland would be setting a foot in his political grave.[35]

As Home Secretary, Jenkins was very reluctant to probe into the situation. He seemed to fear that any thorough investigation of the allegations could have serious constitutional ramifications, which was the last thing he wanted:

> We cannot simply put aside the constitution of Northern Ireland. Successive governments have refused to take any steps which would inevitably cut away not only the authority of the Northern Ireland government but also the constitution of the province.[36]

The evidence that Wilson was committed to acting is perhaps summed up by a comment of his made in 1964: 'Any politician who wants to become involved in Ulster ought to have his head examined.'[37] This attitude was sustained by Wilson due to his apparent view that the Northern Irish Premier Terence O'Neill was a genuine reformer. His view of O'Neill in 1966 was that 'he had already made much progress in a matter of two or three years in attacking problems of discrimination and human rights . . . .'.[38] What evidence was there of this reform? Very little, as the NILP wrote in 1967:

No attempt has been made by the . . . government to knit the community together; there has been no electoral reform, no review of electoral boundaries . . . there is no ombudsman . . . not merely has Captain O'Neill dashed the hopes he himself raised, he has added a new bitterness and disappointment to the grievances of the minority.[39]

Wilson must have been aware of such arguments, but he would not act. When pressed by the London Federation of Trades Councils, who had passed a motion calling for an enquiry into the workings of government in Northern Ireland, Wilson replied,

While the UK Government are wholly opposed to all forms of discrimination, the questions about which allegations of discrimination are made in Northern Ireland fall within the competence of the Northern Ireland authorities. The fact that senior government ministers refused to move on this issue, rendered the CDU's strategy as futile. They later complained that 'letters . . . to Home Secretaries have been treated with contempt'.[40]

The inaction of the leadership was helped by the fact that the CDU never developed into anything approximating a mass movement within the party. Only three constituencies ever affiliated to the organisation. The CDU concluded that Northern Ireland was simply not an attractive proposition for the average British socialist.[41]

The rational arguments of the CDU achieved nothing. Their failure was due to the fact that they failed to understand that the Labour Party was genuinely terrified by the prospect of re-opening the Irish question. The fact that the evidence of discrimination was so clear-cut counted for little in contrast to this. It took the RUC riot in Derry on 5 October 1968 to force Wilson and his colleagues to move. As Paul Rose later recalled,

It was not until millions of television viewers saw a British MP, Gerry Fitt, with his head streaming with blood from a police baton charge that the nation woke up to what some of us in the Commons have been campaigning about month after month in the last five years . . . it is the tragedy of the situation that it was not until heads were broken in London-derry that the attention of the British press, public and parliament were focussed on Northern Ireland.[42]

Conclusion

Ten months later British troops were on the streets of Northern Ireland, where they have remained for twenty years. The failure of the CDU to awaken interest in Northern Ireland during the mid-1960s, even on issues as mainstream as discrimination and civil rights, has a relevance twenty years on. Within British Labour circles, Ireland clearly is an issue apart.

References

1. Interview with Paul Rose MP.
2. *Belfast Newsletter*, 5 October 1964.
3. Paul Bew, Peter Gibbon and Henry Patterson, *The State in Northern Ireland 1921–1972* (Manchester, 1979), p. 190.
4. Geoffrey Bell, *Troublesome Business: The Labour Party and the Irish Question* (London, 1982).
5. Bell, note 4, p. 3.
6. Bell, note 4, p. 9.
7. Barry Stubbs, *The Attitude of the British Labour Party to the Irish Question 1906–1951*, unpublished M. Phil. thesis, University of London.
8. Stubbs, note 7, p. 13.
9. *Hansard*, Vol. 59, Col. 939.
10. Labour Party Conference Report (LPRC), 1920, p. 6.
11. LPRC, 1920 p. 73.
12. LPRC, 1920 p. 23.
13. *Hansard*, Vol. 147, Col. 1407.
14. Bell, note 4, p. 42.
15. Cameron Report, *Disturbances in Northern Ireland* (Belfast, 1969), p. 532.
16. For a full discussion of this, see H. Calvert, *Constitutional Law in Northern Ireland* (London, 1968), pp. 96–97.
17. LPRC, 1926, p. 245.
18. E. Rumpf and A. C. Hepburn, *Nationalism and Socialism in Twentieth-Century Ireland* (Liverpool, 1977), p. 201.
19. For the best account of this, see Bob Purdie, 'The Friends of Ireland: British Labour and Irish Nationalism 1945 to 1949', in Tom Gallagher and J. O'Connell, eds, *Contemporary Irish Studies* (Manchester, 1983).
20. Stubbs, note 7, p. 98.
21. For a full discussion see Ronan Fanning, *Independent Ireland* (Dublin, 1983), pp. 172–80.
22. *Hansard*, Vol. 457, Col. 239.
23. For a full discussion see Bell, note 4, pp. 86–99.

24. Bew, Gibbon and Patterson, note 3, p. 190.
25. Interview with Paul Rose MP.
26. CDU papers 3026/10559.
27. *Hansard*, Vol. 768, Col. 732.
28. Quoted in Paul Rose, 'The Smashing of the Convention', *Irish Times*, 2 March 1970.
29. CDU papers 3026/10559.
30. Interview with Kevin Macnamara MP.
31. CDU papers 3026/10559.
32. Rose, note 28.
33. Interview with Lord Fitt.
34. Interview with Paul Rose MP.
35. Nell McCafferty, 'To Westminster and Back: The Life and Times of Gerry Fitt', *Magill*, July 1983, p. 43.
36. *Hansard*, Vol. 713, Col. 1686.
37. Sunday Times Insight Team, *Ulster* (London, 1972), p. 80.
38. Harold Wilson, *The Labour Government 1964–70* (London, 1974), p. 348.
39. CDU papers 3026/2 10559.
40. CDU papers 3026/2 10559.
41. Interview with Paul Rose MP.
42. LPCR, 1969, p. 177.

6

Women in Northern Ireland: an overview

Monica McWilliams

In presenting an overview of the women's movement in Northern Ireland, this essay will begin by discussing some of the dominant influences on women's lives. The role which both the Church and State play shapes not only the more traditional thinking behind some of the major institutions, such as the education system or the judiciary, but it is also responsible for the extremely conservative ideology for which the Province has become infamous. It is undoubtedly the case that both Church and State have combined together in ensuring that the prime role of women is as mothers and housewives. In the face of such traditional Catholicism and Protestant fundamentalism it has proved extremely difficult for women to organise around issues which are of personal and political importance to them. Feminists when raising issues relating to sexuality, the dissolution of marriage or equal rights in the home or at work, face a good deal more opposition, not only from clergy and politicians, but also from within their own communities. The fact that they have gone some way down this road in organising and politicising around such 'controversial' issues is a testimony to the strength and determination which women here have to drag Ireland kicking and screaming into the twentieth century.[1]

The backwardness of the Northern Irish state can best be seen by the reaction to legislative change in the Province, particularly on issues of sexual morality. The Free Presbyterian Church organised a campaign to 'Save Ulster From Sodomy' to counteract Jeff Dudgeon's case to the European Court in 1982 which resulted in homosexuality being decriminalised. Despite this move, the Catholic Church still holds the view that 'objectively,

Juliet Simmons

homosexual acts are intrinsically and gravely immoral'.[2] Divorce on the grounds of irreconcilability was eventually made legal in Northern Ireland in 1978 – ten years after the rest of Britain. The Democratic Unionist Party, and in particular Ian Paisley, used the 'sanctity of marriage' argument to obstruct the legislation (*Protestant Telegraph*, July 1978). In the end they succeeded in introducing amendments which made 'quickie' postal divorces impossible and divorce itself more expensive. It could only be obtained through High Court proceedings.[3] Such hostility to social change was strongly evidenced not only by the Free Presbyterians but by the Catholic Church. In a *Pastoral Letter* it was argued that

> the concept of irretrievable breakdown in marriage is the basis for the most restrictive form of divorce in the world today. It can be imposed on an innocent and unwilling partner by an unfaithful spouse and the innocent partner can do nothing to prevent it. The remedy for a minority of marriages which fail, itself becomes a factor causing more marriages to fail. A divorce mentality spreads through the community.[4]

In a similar vein to Bowlby's maternal-deprivation thesis of the 1950s, the Bishops argue that 'reliable studies indicate that children prefer even an unhappy marriage relationship to divorce of their parents. Divorce is always a disaster for children'.[5] Such sweeping generalisations were to be taken as fact by the Catholic laity and the 'reliability' of the studies uncontested.

Despite these views, the judiciary had the responsibility of introducing this legislation in July 1978. This was seen as the culmination of many years of campaigning by groups such as the Women's Law and Research Group and the Northern Ireland Women's Rights Movement. Lord Justice McDermott, however, did not share the views of the women's groups. He was more in tune with Church thinking on the subject when he remarked that such laws were 'perils to family life'. (*Belfast Telegraph*, July 1978)

Again in 1980, when the domestic violence legislation was being amended to bring it into line with similar legislation in Britain, the Northern Ireland Assembly adapted it to fit their own particular thinking on the subject. Consequently the 1980 order specified that it should be applied to married couples only and not to cohabitees, since the latter 'chose to live in sin they would have to face the consequences'.[6] Some elements of the Judiciary were once again appalled by the 'perils to family life', this time in the shape of exclusion orders. One local magistrate was forced to adjourn court proceedings, until he read the actual order and was convinced that in his words 'a man could be put out of his own home'.[7] Other barristers recall magistrates speaking of their regret that a time had come once again to Ireland when men could be 'thrown out on to the street'.[8] Not being disposed to understanding the reasons for introducing such legislation on domestic violence, some magistrates in Northern Ireland were erroneously equating exclusion orders with the penal evictions of the nineteenth century.

Interestingly, the issue of domestic violence throws up some contradictions in the Northern Ireland context. Although women protested vociferously against the violence of the British Army throughout the 1970s, particularly at the time of Internment, they were less likely to protest against the violence of their male partners in their own homes. The traditional link between nationalism (both Orange and Green) and their respective Churches has ensured that the ultra-conservative view of women as both the property of, and inferior to, men remains strongly entrenched in Irish society. When the question of domestic violence as a specific campaigning issue arose in the late 1970s in Derry, it brought Women's Aid there into conflict with both the Churches and the Republican Movement. The Church disagreed with the women's campaign to end the cohabitation rule and was initially opposed to the provision of women's refuges on the grounds that they split-up families. The paramilitaries, on the other hand, became angry with the women's group when they refused to distinguish between, on the one hand, violence involved in 'political punishments' (the tarring and feathering of women), and on the other, the violence inflicted by state forces or by husbands.[9]

Over the last twenty years of campaigning and mobilising for social change women here have had to be extra-sensitive to the 'beliefs and traditions' operating in the community. There is a view that to move too quickly down the feminist road, in the light of such Church opposition, may only alienate some women or prevent a more progressive consciousness from developing. Beth Rowland was involved in an education project for women and holds the view that some of the tenets of the feminist movement strike at the very heart of the women's religious beliefs. She questions whether feminists have any right to challenge the traditional role of women since it has so often provided them with their only real identity. She goes further by arguing that these 'religious beliefs are a fact of life which the education/community worker must accept'.[10]

However the majority of politically active women have come up against this hurdle before. Women's groups have begun to enquire about the origins of these religious beliefs. They do not accept that their traditional role within the family, which gives them their only identity as mothers and wives, cannot be changed. It is difficult, often painful, to challenge a set of beliefs which have been so strongly inculcated through the education system. Education in Ireland has an almost adhesive effect between Church, State, women and morality. Inglis quotes from a Parliamentary Commission Report in his book *Moral Monopoly*, 'the civilisation of Irish society depends not just on giving more power to the Catholic Church but on the transformation of Irish women into good mothers'.[11] The Church through the schools became a provider of education while parents became providers of their children as faithful members of the Catholic Church. Not only were Catholic girls to model themselves on the image of the Virgin Mary by maintaining their chastity and purity, but equally they were called upon to adopt the mother's passive, unquestioning role. Mary Holland in particular has commented on this image of motherhood which runs through our popular culture: 'We have apostrophised the country itself as a mother. The concept of Mother Ireland has met with wholehearted national approval. The message has been unequivocal. The proper place for a woman apart from the convent is the home preferably rearing sons for Ireland.'[12]

When the Pope visited Ireland in 1979 his conservative orthodox views on women (not to mention women's rights) became enshrined in his appeal to young Irish women: 'May Irish Mothers, young women and girls not listen to those who tell them that working at a secular job, succeeding in a secular profession is more important than the vocation of giving life and caring for this life as a mother. . . . I entrust this to Mary, bright Sun of the Irish Race'. (Pope John Paul II at Limerick, October 1979) Marina Warner, in her book *Alone of All Her Sex*, traces the history of the Marian devotion.[13] She argues that, by making the virginity of Christ's mother an article of faith, the Church has quite consciously separated sex from motherhood. This is an important distinction and one which many young women in

Ireland are familiar with. In fact Mary Holland holds the view that by passing this philosophy on through the Catholic education system, it has taught Irish women to hate their bodies.[14]

Throughout the late seventies (particularly at the time of the Hunger Strike) wall murals began to appear on the Falls Road in nationalist West Belfast depicting the anguish of Mary as she stands over her martyred son. The pictures were meant to convey a symbol of Mother Ireland where the crucifiers are of course British imperialists. Whilst the Church shows a good deal of antipathy towards such portraits, they do not find it problematic that the Catholic Church, in the form of Virgin Mary, should be represented on the side of the oppressed.

More recently some politically active women in Northern Ireland were asked to discuss what this imagery meant for them. In a banned Channel Four programme, *Mother Ireland*, Bernadette McAliskey saw herself as a 'daughter of Mother Ireland' whilst Mairead Farrell exhorted Mother Ireland 'to get off our backs'.[15] Roisin McDonagh, writing in *Women's News*, argues that she initially had some sympathy with such a rejection, identifying the image with 'a crass, sentimental and ultimately offensive stereotype of Ireland as a tragic but stoically dignified woman whose honour was/is defended by her brave sons fighting against perfidious Albion'.[16] However an identification with the Irish culture and the Gaelic language is beginning to take root amongst a group of feminists in Belfast, and within this, they argue, there is room for different Irish mythological images of the Great Mothers of our culture – images of mothers as warriors, clever, imaginative, strong, cunning, wise and compassionate.[17] Roisin McDonagh argues that these are precisely the ideological images of Mother Ireland trampled down by the imposition of a narrow, patriarchal colonial culture.

In the case of the Protestant Church, the veneration of Mary as a mother figure is anathema to the teachings of Free Presbyterianism. The patriarchal nature of Protestantism leaves out the imagery of women and in turn women become invisible. Where it does refer to women, its more Calvinistic theology calls upon them to be obedient and subservient – again emphasising their prime role as homemakers. This was more noticeable in the post-war period when the State's alignment with the Church helped to institutionalise some of the most extreme forms of patriarchy. Examples of these were investment for male, but not female, employment, the exclusion of women from certain occupations through marriage-bars and the closure of day nurseries. The Ministry of Education refused to take over the well-established and efficiently-run workplace nurseries which had allowed the cheap, yet skilled, labour of married women to be used so profitably in the linen mills. Their labour however was to be expendable since the Stormont administration refused to subvent the linen industry, which would have enabled it to compete with foreign producers. The same rule did not apply to the shipbuilding industry since these men's jobs, which were also predominantly Protestant, had to be protected at all costs.[18] Since the Second World War, the consistently higher levels of unemployment, and the decline in manufacturing industry, encouraged the government in Northern Ireland to pursue a development strategy which would attract investment for male employment. Not only did female workers lose their jobs in the clothing and textile industries, they also lost the possibility for women to combine work, marriage and motherhood. The marriage-bars, operating in the civil service, teaching professions, banking, etc., were not abolished until the late 1960s. These had a profound effect on married women's employment in the Province and undoubtedly help to explain why, in 1971, only 29 per cent of married women were economically active. This contrasts sharply with the figure for Great Britain (42 per cent). Only now, in the mid-to-late eighties, are married women beginning to catch up.[19]

The other major factor which helps to explain the lower economic activity of married women in Northern Ireland is their higher fertility rates. The Province has one of the highest child-dependency ratios in Europe, exceeded within OECD countries only by the Republic of Ireland and Turkey. In 1986 the birth rate was 17.5 births per thousand population compared to 12.5 for Great Britain. As one would expect, family size remains consistently larger and stands unchanged since 1983 at 2.3 children.[20]

Although Protestant family size is greater than the average in Great Britain, it is undoubtedly the case that the number of children in Catholic families is larger than that in Protestant families. However the birth rate for both Protestants and Catholics is declining due to an increasing use of contraception and a demand for females to remain in the labour force. Despite the Catholic Church's strong views on contraception, younger married women in Northern Ireland are making up their own minds.

This does not mean that they are no longer practising Catholics. Contrary to the Church's view that the demands for contraception and sterilisation are a result of 'modern society organised on the basis of sex without control', women are very much in control.[21] As Nell McCafferty believes, Irish women pick and choose with intelligence among the rules drawn up by the Holy Men for the best expression of that belief.[22]

Young people however still have the utmost difficulty in obtaining contraception, as is revealed by the high rates of illegitimacy for women under the age of 20.[23] In 1979, in the Republic of Ireland, 'an Irish solution to an Irish problem' was found in the Health (Family Planning) Act which legalised the distribution and use of contraceptives – but only to persons with *bona fide* family planning purposes.[24] Prior to 1979, many women from the Republic travelled to Northern Ireland to avail themselves of contraceptives. One of the first women's groups in the North (the Socialist Women's Group formed in 1975) highlighted this anomaly by taking a supply of contraceptives to Dundalk (on the Southern side of the border) and freely handing them out. Their mode of transport became known as 'the condom train'.

In 1985 in the Republic of Ireland, the sale of contraceptives was legalised but, as in Northern Ireland, this did not solve the problem. Like sterilisation, and reproductive technology, the availability of contraception depends a great deal on one's social class and place of residence. The problem for women in the North is that although family planning is free, the clinics themselves may not be easily accessible – particularly for those living in rural areas. It is also the case that women, in predominantly Catholic areas, cannot freely obtain contraceptives because doctors will not prescribe them and chemists will not stock them. Single women and men, and married couples who have a social relationship with their doctors, still feel a certain stigma. They know they are deviating from the 'moral' code. Perhaps they are still reeling from the words of the Bishops who as late as 1985 were able to write: 'Every age has had its surfeit of sin, but it can hardly be denied that our contemporary Western society has seen an unprecedented breakdown of what were once universally accepted moral standards, especially in the sphere of sexuality. It is as though our whole civilisation is aphrodisiac.' (*Love is for Life*, Irish Bishops' Pastoral, 1985) To counteract such views feminists have formed supportive collectives around the issues of family planning and women's health. The Well Women's Centre opened in Belfast in 1986 and is used as both an advice centre and pressure group.

Although the Protestant Church does not agree with the Catholic Church's teaching on birth control and divorce, they themselves have not been averse, as we have seen, to enshrining Protestant practice in Northern legislation when the opportunity arose. They are opposed to the extension of the 1967 Abortion Act and, with the Catholic Church, support David Alton's Bill. Their liberality on the issue of birth control may be questioned. 'It often provokes sectarian feeling in that the more ultra-Protestant advocacy of contraception is not posed in terms of women's emancipation but rather stems from a fear of being outbred by feckless Catholics.'[25] It is the case that one of the most sectarian debates in Stormont took place over the allowances paid to families for their children in 1954.[26] The Unionists wished to stop all payments to Catholics with more than four children. Such statements that there 'was little poverty under the blanket' and that 'Catholics breed like rats' often colour such arguments.[27]

The two religious traditions take a similar line on the domestic role of women. They exhort mothers to take responsibility for their children by looking after them at home. The Church feels threatened by the provision of day care for children since it assumes intervention by the State in family life and poses a threat to the concept of the family wage. Childcare, either at the workplace or state-provided, poses a challenge to the traditional ideology which supports the segregated division of labour in the home. Liz McShane shows that in 1945 both Catholic Bishops and Unionist MPs agreed with the closure of day nurseries in the Province, arguing that they destroyed 'the natural and divinely ordained traditional family'. (*Bishops' Lenten Pastoral*)[28] Both class and sex bias is revealed in the lack of understanding of the impoverishment from which women suffer. In preventing women's emancipation by opposing nursery facilities, the Church and State oppressed women by keeping them isolated in the home on a full-time basis. 'The proper place for the baby is in the home and the proper guardian is the mother. Nature decided that and God approved of that decision of Nature.' (Bishop McGean, 1945)[29] The opportunity was lost for a child-centred educational and welfare rationale for day nurseries which would have dramatically increased the opportunities of women to participate in employment. Liam O'Dowd rightly claims that 'the ideology of [Church] intellectuals is largely the product of men who have either ignored or marginalised the social role of women or alternatively consigned women to a servicing and largely invisible role outside history and politics'. It could be argued that by their very exclusion, women in Northern Ireland have been discriminated against. It is less a case of what is said about them, than what is not said. By leaving things alone discrimination occurs in itself because existing models are completely derived from a male representation of reality. This reality Beth Rowland (as noted earlier) interprets as being 'safe' because women know no other. These male perceptions have long shown a determination to preserve the community and family, rather than the individual, as the basic unit of society. In Northern Ireland, models can have a very long life in situations where they are taken as given. Women are now succeeding in challenging their lack of position, their very exclusion from this 'male stream' way of life, and they are having some success in doing so.

However, there still exists a good deal of hysterical negativism from Church and State when women do speak out. On the issue of abortion not only is there a lack of rational debate, but those associated with the campaign are publicly denounced. As the Northern Ireland Abortion Law Reform Association testified to a Tribunal in Belfast in 1987, there is so much fear and secrecy around abortion that women are afraid. The Tribunal itself was aptly titled 'Breaking the Silence'.[30] As a result of the legal situation, certain simple and relatively risk-free ante-natal tests, which are commonly available in Britain, are not routinely offered in Northern Ireland. Because doctors have no clear guidelines under the relevant legislation (1861 Offences Against the Person Act amended by the 1945 Criminal Justice (NI) Act which is the equivalent of the 1929 Infant Life (Preservation) Act in Britain) there are inconsistencies within the medical profession. Where a woman conceives as a result of rape or incest, termination of the pregnancy is left to the doctor's discretion. Abortions are performed, though they are not guaranteed in all such circumstances, and fear of legal reprisal leaves the medical profession unwilling to discuss their practice. Again doctors are often left to impose their own legal and moral judgements upon women. When trade unionists and members of the health and medical professions attempt to raise some of the concerns mentioned above they are reminded that if they are Catholics they should be guided by the tenets of Catholic teaching. Just as

Irish political parties have divided within themselves for religious reasons on moral issues, so have trade union movements, legal organisations, medical professions and even women's groups working in the community. This seems to be one of the major resources of the Church – its capacity to divide other groups whose members give prior allegiance to their religious beliefs. In a similar way many women become so concerned about their family, relatives, friends or neighbours that they do not feel at liberty to betray their religion. The Church uses this as a strategy to avoid social and political change. Whilst applauding the mobilisation of women in the officially-sanctioned Peace Movement, it deplores the organisation of small groups of women around issues of person-concern particularly when they relate to 'sexual morality'. It remains the case that in Ireland the Catholic Church, in putting forward its 'option for the poor', is much more comfortable with Marx than with Freud.[31]

The women's movement in Northern Ireland is making some headway towards social and political change. It is creating structures which enable individuals to have some measure of control over their lives. This is clear particularly in the work of one umbrella organisation known as 'The Women's Information Day'.[32] Other women's groups which deserve credit in this field are Women's Aid, the Women's Education Project and the Northern Ireland Women's Rights Movement. All organise in a non-sectarian way – holding meetings in both nationalist and loyalist areas and raising controversial issues which are sensitive to one another's beliefs. The support of the Protestant working-class women who came together with Catholics in these groups is far from fictitious, a claim which was made by the co-ordinator of the Falls Women's Centre.[33] On one occasion in 1985, while campaigning on changes to the benefit system, a group of Protestant and Catholic women took the Liverpool boat-and-train to London where they lobbied their MPs to oppose the Social Security Bill which was going through Parliament at that time. They were appalled to find that their own political representatives were more interested in opposing the Anglo-Irish Agreement (unfortunately being launched on the same day) and hence refused to meet them on the grounds that they were too busy. The women remained undaunted. Before they left Westminster they successfully lobbied MPs from outside of Northern Ireland by recalling their own personal experiences as claimants. They returned home to Belfast on the same night more convinced than ever that their political representatives were much less interested in matters of social and economic concern.[34]

For women in Northern Ireland one of the most glaring features of life is the hardship of poverty with all its social, financial and psychological repercussions. Everywhere it is good to be at the top of the list in terms of household income, earnings or standards of housing, women in Northern Ireland find themselves at the bottom. Every time it would be preferable to be at the bottom – as indicated by infant mortality rates, unemployment, or dependency on social security – women in Northern Ireland find they have the highest ratings. It is against such a background that the term 'feminisation' of poverty takes its meaning. It is women who experience poverty as prisoner's wives, as widows, as single parents, divorced, separated or unmarried, as managers of unemployed families, as single and elderly women living alone, or as low-paid wage earners.[35] For the majority, it is both humiliating and degrading. In attempting to combat this, many local-community women's groups have now started offering advice and information to women. The Northern Ireland Women's Rights Movement has produced thousands of simple self-explanatory leaflets enabling this process to take place and helping to empower women in the face of overwhelming bureaucracy. Existing from day to day in the North can often become an intolerable strain for women. Not only must they provide a reasonable standard of living for their kids, but they have the additional anxiety of worrying about husbands and children when they are out of the home. The years of 'the troubles' have added to their pressures and many respond by using tranquilisers or smoking excessively.[36]

It is women who have led the anti-poverty campaigns – a politically significant role which is often ignored by the media, church leaders and politicians. Kate Kelly makes the interesting point that the Women's Information Day group refused to let single individuals (or political parties) become solely identified with their campaigns.[37] Their non-hierarchical structure proved time and again to be the supportive environment the women required. Each became knowledgeable about the issue under scrutiny, confidence and experience were gathered together, and often the women maintained links after the campaign had been dissolved.

One important feature of this organisation, as today with many local and trade-union women's groups, is the importance of a creche. The women cannot have a productive meeting if the kids are not adequately minded. The NI Women's Rights Movement now provides a 'Rent-a-Creche' (or mobile unit) which facilitates women's groups and enables outreach work in the community. The neglect of the importance of minding small infants and babies is revealed by the fact that Rent-a-Creche are frequently offered toilets or changing rooms for facilities when the groups are holding meetings in leisure or community centres.

Like women everywhere, women in Northern Ireland have developed interests and confidence through traditional associations such as mother-and-toddler groups, budgeting and benefit classes. Although initially dubbed 'family feminists' (because of their altruistic concern with husbands and sons) the Women's Information Day group, with many other community groups, has avoided the risk of the containment of women. These women's groups have provided a necessary means of gathering support for women's issues and have initiated campaigns on questions which have community validity.

From the civil rights days of the late sixties and early seventies, to the organisation of campaigns, community projects and women's centres in the mid-seventies and eighties, feminists in Northern Ireland have played a central role. A great deal has been learned along the way. Initially, in the civil rights movement, men and women marched together demanding 'One Man, One Vote'. The chant was given without any consideration to its sexist connotations. Only later were the women able to reflect on this. Such a slogan would be unheard of today. It was in the civil rights movement that some of the women cut their political teeth. It was female students at Queen's University in April 1975 who held the first public meeting which helped to form an action group 'with the aim of bringing the role of women in Northern Ireland into line with that of their sisters in Britain'. (*Belfast Telegraph,* 28 April 1975) This same group soon became the NI Women's Rights Movement and its first campaign was successfully to bring the Sex Discrimination Act to Northern Ireland. Although a split occurred with the Socialist Women's Group over the question of anti-imperialism, there are still many issues around which women's groups in Northern Ireland find common ground. Probably because the country is so small many women know and readily acknowledge the political affiliations of those with whom they work. Similarly, it is not uncommon for a woman here to be active in her women's group, her trade union and her local community so that a good deal of cross-over occurs on various issues making the lobbying of political parties and/or statutory bodies much easier. Unlike the situation in Britain, however, women's groups receive little official recognition and much less funding.

As a consequence of their grass-roots involvement trade-union women have established an extremely healthy relationship between the Irish Congress of Trade Unions (Northern Ireland Committee) and the Northern Ireland Women's Rights Movement. The ICTU is affiliated to the Women's Rights Movement in Belfast – something which might be considered unlikely for the TUC in London! Different styles of working are, of course, operated by the two very different organisations. The Women's Rights Movement tends to be less formally structured and a good deal more spontaneous in its campaigning and advice work, whilst it benefits from the direct negotiations which the ICTU has from time to time with various government ministers. This symbiotic relationship was best revealed during the past two years of the ICTU's anti-sectarian campaign 'Peace, Work and Progress'. Female trade unionists became particularly active in this, holding meetings of local women in various towns throughout Northern Ireland. Equally, on the issue of strip-searching, women's conference resolutions meant that ICTU officials were asked to negotiate with Nicholas Scott (then the Minister responsible for HM prisons in Northern Ireland).[38]

It is important finally to examine some of the issues which divide feminists in the Women's Movement. They are mostly related to the 'National Question' which still haunts many women in Northern Ireland. Whether they are single issue women's groups such as Women's Aid or the Rape and Incest Line, or generic groups such as the Derry, Belfast or the Falls Road Women's Centres, the political affiliations of the members may be surreptitiously guaged in order to clarify the line they might take on the National Question. This might never be discussed in the day-to-day running of the organisation, or, if already established, it may be deliberately ignored to avoid confrontation. But this should not be interpreted as an attempt to silence republicans (or indeed loyalists). What it means is that different women's groups adopt different tactics when raising the issue of partition. In Northern Ireland it would be difficult for any women's group to assume the exclusive prerogative to speak on the National Question. Disputes have occurred between the

Relative's Action Committee and Women Against Imperialism (which predominantly support Sinn Fein) and other women's groups such as the Belfast Women's Collective and the NI Women's Rights Movement. The Belfast Women's Collective (formed in 1977) argued that it was 'vital to work in as wide a range as possible, including [areas] which may not initially meet with a big response because they challenge traditional political and religious beliefs'. (*Women's Action* May/June 1978) The Relative's Action Committee, organising around the withdrawal of political status from the H Block Maze Prison, took the view that the campaign about the prisons (particularly on behalf of the women in Armagh Prison) should be central. They argued that imperialism is the major dominating force in the lives of women throughout Ireland and specifically the women in West Belfast. (*Women's Action*, June 1978)[39] Whether or not the National Question is the dominant feature in working-class women's lives remains a thorny subject.

Christina Loughran argues that those feminists who gave up their autonomy to go into Sinn Fein have made real gains in terms of the policies adopted. One of the gains to which she refers is the 'women's right to choose' which Sinn Fein as a Party had opposed until 1985. However, Sinn Fein remains reluctant publicly to acknowledge this in its manifestos – particularly in the recent local government elections of June 1989. It is interesting to note that Sinn Fein once castigated the NI Women's Rights Movement for seeking extensions to British legislation on divorce and abortion on the grounds that they were imperialistic reforms and diluted the struggle.[40] It took a major effort by feminists to challenge the often patriarchal and reactionary attitudes to women which have characterised the Nationalist Movement. Marie Mulholland makes an insightful contribution to a debate with which many feminists are familiar. She argues that much of the experience of women in anti-imperialist and Republican organisations is that of having to subjugate their needs as women for the good of the greater cause.[41]

Despite these divisions in the Women's Movement, which are bound to occur, it remains the case that the oppression caused by the present political impasse is deeply destructive to all women. Some are psychologically scarred by the deaths or injuries to loved ones. Some are emotionally burnt-out now the twentieth anniversary – 11 August 1989 – of the presence of armed troops on the street has passed. Women on both sides have faced the destruction of family life when family members are arrested under the emergency Prevention of Terrorism Act, tried by Diplock (non-jury) courts, or held for long periods without trial on remand. Women are subjected to the humiliating and degrading treatment of strip-searching, and women like Emma Groves have been blinded by plastic bullets. Life becomes cheap when joy-riding represents a good time. Over thirty children have been killed either crashing stolen cars or being shot by the army. Women live in fear for their children: that they will be caught in cross-fire, caught-up in a riot, or be blown-up in an explosion. Living in the insidious atmosphere of sectarianism and violence, women on a daily basis have to endure the incessant barking of patrol and guard dogs and the continuous birr of army helicopters. These multiple layers of oppression affect all women in Northern Ireland. Some damage women living in Nationalist areas more, while others affect Catholic and Protestant equally. These are some of the major issues which feminists have had to tackle, alongside their struggle against economic exploitation and sexual oppression.

The women's movement in Northern Ireland has a daunting task, particularly in the aftermath of the Anglo-Irish Agreement and the recent display of conservative sexism in both Britain and Ireland.[42] In the process many Catholic as well as Protestant women have been further alienated, but the women's movement in general is actively striving to create a politics which challenges the conservativism of the Northern State, as well as the Southern, and the male-dominated ideas of the governing Churches. Some progress has been made on the question of equal opportunity. Legislation has been introduced which will monitor workforces for evidence of discrimination on grounds of religion and sex. Interestingly the Equal Opportunities Commission, which is known to play a much more active role in women's lives than its GB counterpart, was almost abolished in Northern Ireland.[43] As a consequence of lobbying and submissions from trade-union and community women, the EOC continues to function and provide support for a wide variety of women's groups in the Province. Twenty years on, questions of religious and sexual discrimination remain just as pertinent. In their efforts to allay American fears about Catholic male unemployment, the Northern Ireland Office needs constant reminders that women face the double exploitation of both their sex and their religion. In an effort to raise women's issues beyond the backyard conservativism of

Northern Ireland, women are now organising into a network directly to lobby the European Commission. As we move towards 1992, some answers have to be found to the questions about why Northern Ireland does not move nearer to the position of other European countries on issues involving sexual morality and women's rights. The lack of any liberal-democratic representation does make the task more politically difficult for the women's movement. There is a feeling, however, that as we have laid the ground for political and social change to take place, there is a new generation of younger women who are prepared directly to take-up the challenge and speak for themselves. It is their view that Church and State will no longer control women's lives, as they did in the past, or so blatantly obstruct women's rights. In the Trade Union Movement, the Student's Union and the wider community, women are negotiating a new agenda. The question of partition will undoubtedly continue to create internal and external divisions amongst women's groups. It is too much to expect that there will not be these differences, or that relations will always be healthy. Learning to respect each other, and to prioritise differently, has long been a feature of the women's movement. It is to the credit of women's groups such as the NI Women's Rights Movement, the Women's Education Project and the Women's Information Day that they have 'stayed the course' against all odds. They have recognised that mobilisation around issues of social emancipation and economic advancement can in turn lead to movement on issues of democratic rights and of national liberation. Moreover, they have crossed traditional boundaries and drawn women from all sections of the working class into these struggles. Any categorisation of such a strategy as 'reformist' invariably attempts to dismiss the progressive advances that they have made.[44] It will be the case, though, that when men and women sit down to design the constitution for a New Ireland (if there will ever be such a thing), then the women's movement will have ensured its right to be included. The role of women will be central and not marginal in such discussions. Women have endured too much for that to happen again.

References

1. Gemma Hussey used this phrase frequently during speeches as a Minister in the Coalition Government in the Irish Republic in the late 1970s.

2. Irish Bishops' Pastoral Letter, *Love Is For Life*, (April 1985), p. 9.
3. This was later amended in 1984, mainly due to demand and the back-log of cases at the Belfast High Court.
4. Irish Bishops' Pastoral Letter, note 2, p. 9.
5. Irish Bishops' Pastoral Letter, note 2, p. 5.
6. From accounts by workers in NI Women's Aid recalling the debate in the Northern Ireland Assembly over the 1980 legislation. The legislation was later amended to have cohabitees included. The situation on domestic violence is now similar to legislative provision in Great Britain.
7. Interview with J. McGettrick, Belfast solicitor, speaking about his first case under the new legislation.
8. Interview with Madge Davidson, barrister, recalling her work in the Magistrates' Courts.
9. Cathy Harkin and Avilla Kilmurray in M. Abbott and H. Frazer, eds., *Women in Community Work* (Belfast, 1985).
10. Beth Rowland in Abbot and Frazer, note 9.
11. T. Inglis, *Moral Monopoly* (Dublin, 1987).
12. Mary Holland, *Irish Times*, 20 February 1988.
13. Marina Warner, *Alone Of All Her Sex* (London, 1985).
14. Mary Holland, note 12.
15. A. Crilly, *Mother Ireland* (Derry Film and Video Workshop). The film was scheduled to be televised on Channel Four but was never shown following the death of Mairead Farrell in Gibraltar.
16. Roisin McDonagh, review of Marie Mulholland, ed., *Unfinished Revolution* (Belfast, 1989) in *Women's News*, April 1989.
17. Noirin Ni Cleirigh, Nuala Ni Dhomhnaill and others involved in 'Women in Irish Culture' Workshop, Conway Mill, March 1989.
18. Hazel Morrissey in M. Morrissey, ed., *Unemployment, The Other Crisis* (Ulster Polytechnic Occasional Papers, 1980).
19. *Regional Trends* (1987). The 1985 figures were 52 per cent for Great Britain and 45 per cent for Northern Ireland. For a more extensive discussion see M. McWilliams et al., *EOC Report*, (1989).
20. 1.9 children is the equivalent figure in Great Britain.
21. Irish Bishops' Pastoral Letter, note 2.
22. Nell McCafferty in Marie Mulholland, ed., note 16, p. 16.
23. The illegitimacy rate for women under 20 years is 50 per cent. In 1986 538 out of 1000 live births were recorded as illegitimate. HMSO *Social Trends*, (1987).
24. Phrase coined by Charles Haughey, Taoiseach, to describe Irish family planning (1979).
25. M. T. McGivern and M. Ward in *Images Of Women In Northern Ireland* Crane Bag (1982).
26. For earlier debates see J. Ditch, *Social Policy In Northern Ireland 1939–50* (Avebury, 1988).
27. Board of Guardians in P. Devlin, *Yes We Have No Bananas* (Belfast,

1984). Eddie McAteer, the Stormont Nationalist MP in the fifties responded to this by suggesting that Catholics in turn should take all the benefits to which they were entitled and not concern themselves with any allegiance to the British Welfare State as a consequence of claiming. J. Biggs Davison commented that Catholics were prepared to accept the half-crown but not the Crown.

28. L. McShane, 'Day Nurseries in Northern Ireland 1941–1955' in C. Curtin et al., eds., *Gender in Irish Society* (Galway, 1987).

29. L. McShane, note 28.

30. Northern Ireland Abortion Law Reform Association, *Abortion in Northern Ireland, The Report of an International Tribunal* (Pale Publications, 1989).

31. Rev. Sean Healey, Sr. Brigid Reynolds, 'The Christian Churches and the Poor' in E. Hanna, ed., *Poverty In Ireland* (Social Study Conference, 1987).

32. Women's Information Day meets on the first Tuesday of each month in Catholic and Protestant (or neutral) venues alternately. Between 70 to 100 women attend these meetings.

33. Oonagh Marron, 'The Cost of Silencing Voices like Mine' in Marie Mulholland, note 16.

34. This lobby was organised by the Northern Ireland Women's Rights Movement as part of the protests against the White Paper on Social Security, November 1986.

35. McGivern and Ward, note 25, claim that 35 million tranquillisers are used in Northern Ireland each year and that twice as many women as men are dependent.

36. For a lengthier discussion see M. McWilliams, 'Poverty in Northern Ireland' in E. Hanna, note 31.

37. In the early seventies, Joyce McCartan (now in Women's Information Day) and Lynda Edgerton (now in Northern Ireland Women's Rights Movement) won the support of the Irish Farmers' Association when they led a cow around the City Hall in Belfast to protest against the abolition of school milk for children.

38. ICTU Women's Conference, Malahide 1986. In April 1986 representatives of the Northern Ireland Committee (ICTU) met with Nicholas Scott and the Northern Ireland Office at Stormont Castle to negotiate over the issue of strip-searching when the women were being moved from Armagh Jail to the new prison at Magheraberry. Female prisoners were not strip-searched when the move took place.

39. *Women's Action* was the newsletter of the Belfast Women's Collective. It is now defunct. A different newsletter, *Women's News*, began in 1985 in Belfast and is still in operation.

40. Minutes of the Northern Ireland Women's Rights Movement, 1976.

41. Marie Mulholland in 'Unfinished Revolution', note 16.

42. The Pro-Amendment campaign in the Republic of Ireland in 1983 made abortion unconstitutional and the 1985 Referendum on

Divorce was defeated. In Britain examples would be the Alton Bill on abortion and the Gillick camapign on contraception.

43. The question of religious discrimination dominated the legislation, with issues concerning sex discrimination and equal opportunities taking second place.

44. Christina Loughran has used the term 'Reformist' in her analysis of feminism in Northern Ireland in *Trouble And Strife*, 11 (1988).

7

Economic change and the position of women in Northern Ireland

Hazel Morrissey

Introduction

The purpose of this essay is to set out the relationship between economic change in Northern Ireland and the social position of women. It attempts to set out some of the main issues that affect the current and future agendas for women in the region. The essential context is the magnitude of economic restructuring that has taken place in Northern Ireland both in the recent past, and that which is yet to come with the changes associated with a single European market after 1992. It is alongside this restructuring that new ideas about the role of women have developed. As women become more economically independent, their traditional passivity is eclipsed by a new sense of responsibility and aspirations for a more active role.

This raises other questions about the status of Northern Ireland as a place apart. Is this especially true for women? Do they occupy a place apart, either from each other, or from their counterparts in Britain and Ireland? What are the economic criteria which create the divisions? Can a new Northern Irish identity be built for women around the fact that they are much closer to each other economically than to either of their counterparts in the Irish Republic or Britain?

It also suggests wider considerations about Northern Ireland, not only as a place apart from Britain and the rest of Ireland, but also within the context of Europe. Its peripheral status has important implications for the future. The increasing drive for

Paul Pickersgill

economic centralisation creates a double uneveness of development both within the peripheral regions of the EC, and between the richer and poorer social groups within the regions themselves. The possibilities of the Single European Act (SEA) also concern the development of new European ideas and approaches to confront the world of the 1990s, and women's place as being multi-dimensional within that world. The issues encompass the possible limits to campaigning for equality, the dangers of bigger and better capitalist development and how we articulate and shape the changing perceptions and opportunities.

The article is divided into three parts: the economic position of women in Northern Ireland and a comparative analysis with Britain and the Irish Republic; the economic and social challenges of European integration; and some new thinking on women's future role in the search for a better world. The article does not dwell on the political and sectarian divisions which do obviously mark out Northern Ireland as a place apart, because this is covered elsewhere. These divisions are dealt with only as they affects women in the labour market, where religion is still a powerful variable for males but increasingly less so for females.

The economic context

The shape of Northern Ireland's industrial structure has been transformed from one where the older traditional industries were totally dominant to a newly-emerging landscape where the features are not yet clearly defined. As older traditional industries decline they are being replaced with new sectors dominated by smaller workplaces and high technology.

The old Northern Ireland formed part of an industrial triangle with Scotland and North West England sharing the industries of engineering, shipbuilding and textiles. Women had their own place in this structure, predominating in the linen industry, which at its height was the largest in the world. The industrial revolution in Ireland was built on the linen trade and female labour. During the inter-war period there were two female linen workers for every one male employed in shipbuilding.[1] According to the 1931 Census, women accounted for 37% of the insured population, and during the Second World War women were involved in every traditional male occupation, from train driving to rivetting.

It was only in the post-war situation that opportunities for

Table 1 Female employment in Northern Ireland, June 1982–September 1988

Industrial classification	1982	% of total	1988	% of total
Agriculture	890	10.0	3140	16.3
Energy & Water	1200	12.5	1100	13.4
Extraction, Mftr of Metals & Chemicals	1130	10.8	1550	15.2
Engineering	6580	18.9	6250	20.5
Other Manufacture	29090	45.6	29790	47.6
Manufacturing subtotal	36800	33.8	37630	36.3
Construction	1870	7.1	2500	10.1
Distribution, Hotels, Catering	37820	50.5	43710	52.4
Transport & Communication	3590	18.5	4050	21.0
Banking, Finance	12390	48.3	15560	51.7
Other Services	120710	60.4	128530	61.5
Services subtotal	174510	54.6	19180	56.1
Total	215280	45.5	236220	47.4

women to find paid employment began to contract. This was because linen was the first part of the manufacturing base to decline, leaving women without their traditional occupations of spinning and weaving. When the replacement man-made fibre industry, which was dependent on foreign-owned companies, began to boom in the 1960s and 70s, it was mostly men who were employed as the knitters and weavers, while the cultural imagery of 'latch-key' children fostered a hostile environment for the working wife. The withdrawal of these multinationals from Northern Ireland, following the oil price shock of the early 1970s, coincided with the growth of public services especially after Direct Rule and the election of British Labour governments. And it was to the public sector that women turned for employment opportunities. The women, who traditionally would have worked in manufacturing, now found jobs as cleaners, cooks, dinner ladies and catering assistants. Those women with higher educational qualifications entered the public sector professions as teachers, social workers, lecturers and community workers.

Table 2 The religious structure of economically active females

	Catholics	%	Protestants	%
Unemployed	10,105	17.1	12,775	9.6
Self employed	1,103	1.9	3,185	2.4
Employees	47,795	81.0	116,425	87.9

Source: 1981 Census of Population[5]

As the decline of the traditional manufacturing base continued and demand for labour in services increased, women's share of total employment also grew. By 1988 women accounted for 47% of all employees. Women now form the majority of employees in hotels and catering, retail and distribution, banking, finance and business services, and throughout the public sector. Interestingly they are also beginning to increase their share of manufacturing employment as well, from 33% in 1982 to 36% in 1988.

This changing industrial structure has also altered the occupations of women. By 1985 almost 70% of working women in Northern Ireland were in only three occupational groups: professional and related in education, welfare and health; clerical and related; and catering, cleaning, hairdressing and other professional services.[3] This reflects the importance of the service sector in female employment and also points to their concentration in a few occupations with divergent status and earning power.

The religious factor in female economic activity

The factor of religion is still a very important one in determining employment structures. A recent study by the Fair Employment Agency based on the 1981 Population Census clearly identified the disadvantaged position of Catholics within the Northern Ireland labour market. However while there is continuity of this disadvantage, there has also been some overall improvement. Catholics generally, but especially females and the younger age groups, are beginning to move out of their traditional core occupations and industries.[4]

The unemployed ratio (Table 2) is probably the strongest indicator of disadvantage, but also the fact that Catholic females are less inclined to be self-employed points to a lack of investment

Table 3   Female occupation by religion

	Protestant %	Catholic %
Manual	34.2	33.5
Non-manual	55.9	48.8
Unemployed	9.9	17.7

Source: 1981 Census of Population[5]

capital and the traditional under-representation of Catholic entrepreneurs.

Regarding class profiles there is evidence that all females are under-represented in all positions of authority, which indicates the overall structure of disadvantage of women in the labour market. However, there has been a rapid expansion of females holding non-manual supervisory jobs. In the Greater Belfast area, Catholic females outnumber Protestant females in non-manual supervisory jobs, apprenticeships and other categories of employment, but display a significantly lower percentage in management positions. The percentage for professional employees in Greater Belfast is the same for females of both religions.

Slightly more Protestant women were employed in manual occupations, and they were also over-represented in non-manual occupations. This is a reflection of their higher levels of economic activity generally.(Table 3) Catholic women rely heavily on the public sector for employment; within all industrial divisions they were most visible in the public sector. This accounted for 59% of Catholic female employment compared to 49% of Protestant female employment.

As professional workers Catholic females are concentrated in teaching and nursing where they represent 18% of total employment in education, compared to 13% for Protestants, and 19% in medical and health services compared to 13% for Protestant females. Catholics do less well in the occupations of doctors, dentists, pharmacists and university lecturers.

However, while Catholic females have obviously benefitted from the expansion of professional services within the public sector, they have succeeded to a lesser degree in the private sector. Protestant females have taken most advantage of the expansion of security and protective services where, primarily for political reasons, they outnumber Catholic females by eight to one. Catholic females are also under-represented in banking, insurance and business services, and at all skill levels in the manufacturing sectors of metal engineering and vehicle industries. This probably reflects the older patterns of Protestant employment in such industries.

Manual Catholic females are concentrated in the clothing and textile industries. Many of these industries are located west of the River Bann where Catholic unemployment is highest and other employment opportunities are much lower compared to the more urban eastern areas around Greater Belfast.

Female earnings in Northern Ireland

The structure of female earnings in Northern Ireland has certain key characteristics which have resulted from these changing industrial and occupational patterns. The female earnings distribution will be examined for internal differences and will also be compared with female earnings in other regions and male earnings in this region. It is not possible to analyse earnings by religion because of the lack of data, but certain inferences can be drawn from the general patterns of industrial and occupational pay levels.

Female earnings in 1988

The average weekly pay of full-time working women in Northern Ireland in 1988 was £141 a week. The average pay of non-manual

Table 4   Increases in female earnings, 1987–88 (£)

	1988 Manual	% increase since 1987	1988 Non-Manual	% increase since 1987
Including absence				
Including Overtime	102.6	−0.09	161.4	9.6
Excluding Overtime	98.7	1.1	157.6	9.2
Excluding absence				
Including Overtime	110.4	3.5	163.8	9.6
Excluding Overtime	106.1	5.0	159.9	9.3

Source: New Earnings Survey 1988[6]

Table 5 Distribution of female earnings, 1988 (£)

Gross weekly earnings	Manual	Non-Manual	All
Lowest 10% earned less than	75.8	86.2	80.5
Middle 50% earned less than	106.4	147.4	129.9
Top 10% earned more than	149.2	264.7	247.0

Source: New Earnings Survey 1988[7]

women was £164 and £102 for manual women. Because opportunities for overtime and bonuses are more restricted for women, such payments represented only 4% of manual earnings and 2% of non- manual earnings. The highest rise in average earnings was for non- manual females who increased their pay by 9.6%. Manual females whose pay was affected by absence had no increase at all.

There is a growing divergence between the pay of manual and non-manual female workers. In 1988 there was an average difference of £59 a week compared to £45 in 1987. In percentage terms this means that the gap between manual earnings and non-manual earnings has grown from 30% in 1987 to 57% in 1988.

There is a very wide differential between the high earning, non-manual females and the low paid, manual females, a difference of £189 a week. All the indications are that this is a growing trend. For example, in 1987 the lowest female decile was 81% of the female median, by 1988 this had fallen to 78%. Conversely, the highest earners were paid 178% of the median in 1987 and by 1988 this had risen to 190%.

This widening earnings inequality among women is a reflection of female employment and occupations. The low-paid, manual and non-manual females are working in hotels and catering, the clothing, textile and food-processing industries, and also on small family farms. The bottom occupational categories are clustered around selling, personal services and machine operation. The highest-paid women work in the public sector, business services and the security industry. The best-paid occupations are managerial, the professions in health and education and security personnel.[8]

The fact that non-manual women are increasing their earnings faster than any other group is in part a consequence of the work of the EOC and progress on the equal pay and sex discrimination legislation. It is also a reflection of the predominance of women in the public sector, their entry into the professions and the continuation of career paths after marriage and children.[9] Another important factor for this group is the national character-istics of pay bargaining. Pay structures in the public sector are more reflective and responsive to the higher earnings in Britain and do not take into account regional variations. With regard to the religious factor, the manual/non-manual variable is a more significant indicator of difference than religion. Non-manual women, whether they are Catholics in public sector professions or Protestant women in banking and business services, are significantly improving their position relative to blue-collar females, whether they be Catholic women in the clothing industries, or those Protestant women in the smaller engineering factories. Within the higher-paying occupations, Catholic fe-males are over-represented in the public sector professions while Protestant females dominate in the security industries and private business services. In the low-paying jobs Catholics are more likely to be found in the ancillary sectors of the public sector, while Protestant women are more numerous in hotels, catering and distribution. Of course this is not to deny that there is an overall structure of disadvantage for Catholics which is due primarily to unemployment. But for those women in work there is a growing trend towards harmonisation of opportunity es-pecially in the Greater Belfast area.

In the sense of women being in a place apart from each other economically, it is clear that there are very real distinctions between working women within Northern Ireland. Surprisingly, perhaps, it is the pay differentials that are the real separating factor, and although this is also cut across by a sectarian division, religion is only a secondary indicator of disadvantage.

Comparisons with the rest of the UK

If women in Northern Ireland live the reality of division within the Province, how do they compare with the economic position of women in Britain? Although the changes in the industrial base have mirrored those in Britain (i.e. the recession in the early 1980s created a shake-out in manufacturing), the decline in Northern Ireland was much swifter. The composition of the public sector is

Table 6   Female service sector employment in the UK, 1987

Industry	Percentages of total employment			
	England	Scotland	Wales	N. Ireland
Distribution Hotels, Catering	24.7	26.3	25.5	18.8
Transport Communication	3.0	1.8	2.4	1.6
Banking, Finance	12.1	8.1	9.6	6.3
Public Admin., etc.	41.8	45.0	45.3	54.8
All Services	81.6	81.2	82.8	81.5

Source: Regional Trends 1988[10]

Table 7   Female manufacturing employment in the UK, 1987

Industry	Percentages of total employment			
	England	Scotland	Wales	N. Ireland
Metals, Minerals, Chemicals	1.9	2.1	1.0	0.6
Metal Goods, Engineering	4.9	4.7	4.0	2.6
Other Manufacturing	8.8	9.1	9.4	12.5

Source: Regional Trends 1988[11]

also larger due first of all to the security situation, and also to expanding social services which had lagged behind Britain for so long under the Stormont government.

In all four regions of the UK women are overwhelmingly concentrated in services, though Northern Ireland women are less represented in private services. (Table 5) With regard to manufacturing, females in Northern Ireland are more likely to be concentrated in the 'Other Manufacturing' category. This includes textiles, clothing, food, drink and tobacco.

Thus women in Northern Ireland are still to be found in the 'light' manufacturing industries. Their exclusion from 'heavy' industries remains greater than elsewhere. In 1988 white-collar women in Northern Ireland were the second highest paid in the UK. Their earnings were £163.80 – second only to the South East at £197.80 and followed by the North West at £162.40. However, manual women in Northern Ireland were the worst paid in the UK, using the same category as above they earned an average of

£110.40 compared to the next worst region, South Yorkshire on £112.80 a week.[12]

It is clear therefore that the differentials in female earnings are more significant in Northern Ireland than in other regions of the UK. Even a declining region in Britain like Merseyside, which has economic problems similar to those in Northern Ireland, (high unemployment, low GDP and a large benefit-dependent population) achieved average manual female earnings of £124 in 1988. This was despite the fact that female long-term unemployment is higher than in Northern Ireland, 19% compared to 17%.[13]

Comparisons with the Irish Republic

Although the participation of women in the Irish labour force is increasing, at 32% it is still the lowest in Europe. Women predominate in the sectors of professional and personal services, but are a lower proportion in every other category including retail and business services, whereas in Northern Ireland they also dominate these areas. Those industries employing 5000 or more women are primary education, hospitals, hairdressing and textiles.[14] However, they are well represented in the electronics industries where they constitute 31% of the workforce. A large number of women work in agriculture and 11% of farms are headed by a woman. Many more women whose work is unwaged are married to farmers.[15] The main occupations in which women are employed are clerks, shop assistants, nurses, teachers, typists and maids. Other occupations in which more than 5000 women are employed are nuns, stitchers, waitresses and electronic operatives.[16] As far as pay levels in the Irish Republic are concerned average female earnings in 1988 were £146 a week compared to £246 for males. Unlike Northern Ireland, manual occupations in manufacturing can be highly paid: average earnings for women in office and data-processing machinery production were £187 a week and £183 for drink and tobacco.[17] There is no comparative data on non-manual earnings. In fact no direct comparisons can be made between Northern Ireland and the Irish Republic because first of all their PAYE tax structure is much more punitive, starting at 31% and increasing sharply as earnings grow, and secondly the higher cost of living and VAT rates lowers purchasing power.[18] The structures of the two economies in Ireland differ considerably, and although women are entering the labour force in greater numbers, the

Table 8   Female earnings in relation to male
earnings, Northern Ireland, 1988 (£)

	Males	*Females*	*Females as a % of males*
Manual	167.6	102.5	61.6
Non-Manual	263.8	161.4	61.1
All	210.1	141.4	67.3

Source New Earnings Survey 1988[19]

nature of Irish society and lack of employment opportunities are
the restraining factors. However, the European context of 1992
and the reality of the peripheral areas may bring women from
North and South closer together, both economically and in
campaigning organisations for a political voice.

Female and male earnings in Northern Ireland

The evidence so far suggests that there is a growing gap in the
earning power of different groups of women. How do all earning
levels of females relate to their male counterparts? The high-
paying non-manual female earnings and the low-paid manual
male earnings meant that in 1986 the ratio of female to male
earnings in Northern Ireland was the highest in the UK at 70%
compared to 66% in all other regions. However this tends to
obscure the fact that there is still a wide difference between male
and female earnings.

The evidence presented here suggests that the industrial and
occupational recomposition that has accompanied economic
change in Northern Ireland has had a fundamental impact on
female employment and earnings. More women are entering
paid employment than ever before. Employers are now displaying an active preference for female labour and the flexibility it
offers in terms of work arrangement. In terms of remuneration,
non-manual females continue to improve their earnings position,
to maintain comparable earnings with similar groups in Britain
and to obtain a greater proportion of male earnings. By no means
have they achieved equality, but their position relative to manual
females is substantially better. By contrast, the latter group have
fared very badly; they have failed to retain their earnings level

and are falling further behind all other groups of workers. In 1987/88 they suffered real earnings decline, and the danger lies in them becoming a source of even cheaper labour as competition increases.

The European dimention – the challenge of 1992

The Single European Act had its origins in the concern of the European Parliament to investigate the slow-down in the European economies relative to America and Japan. Various studies found that EC states had responded to the oil crisis by protecting their own national economies from competition from other member states.[20] They did this not through import controls, but by imposing complex technical specifications on products to be retailed within their own markets. Another contributory factor was that Europe had not invested in high technology to the same extent as its two rivals. The European Parliament concluded from these reports that the principle cause of this slow-down was the failure to develop full economic integration. In other words by the early eighties Europe had run out of steam, finding it difficult to compete as a trading area and constantly bickering over protracted budgetry disputes. Public opinion had lost interest in Europe and was growing increasingly hostile to the whole idea.

The promise of a single market after 1992 has certainly given the EC a shot in the arm as business and social organisations try to come to terms with what it will mean for them. The reality of common standards of taxation and currency and the complete freedom of movement of labour, capital, and all forms of trade is difficult to anticipate. With the removal of economic tariffs at all ports and borders, frontiers between member states will gradually be eliminated. The advocates of 1992 point to rapid gains in technology, increasing employment and lower prices.

However, this appears to be over-optimistic, especially for peripheral regions like Northern Ireland. The effects of economic integration tend to concentrate capital and resources not only into individual companies which are the largest and most advanced, but also into areas which have the facilities to service the needs of these powerful interests. After 1992 manufacturing industry, financial services and political administration will be concentrated more and more at the centre of Europe, in Belgium, France, Germany, the Benelux countries, southern England, and northern Italy.

Northern Ireland stands as a place apart from this so-called 'golden triangle', and faces the prospect of 1992 reinforcing the trend associated with the region's decline. For example, the average size of Northern Ireland industry is very small; over 70% of companies employ less than twenty, and 60% only serve the local market.[21] It is predicted that half of Europe's small firms will close after 1992 in the battle for increased market shares.

The impact on women in Northern Ireland of these massive economic and social changes that are occuring cannot be precisely predicted. There are new opportunities opening up, coupled with the negative effects of economic restructuring. Demographic changes and a falling birth-rate will mean a 20% reduction in the numbers of school leavers by 1995.[22] There is a growing recognition among employers of the need to retain skilled female labour and to tempt older women back into the labour market to fill these gaps. However 1992 will mean different things to women in different social categories. Those who are young, mobile, educated and with language skills will find many new opportunities both within Europe and in Northern Ireland. Professional women will gain from the new harmonisation of qualifications, which means the ability to take jobs in other member states without the need for additional retraining.

On the other hand, the prospects for women at the bottom end of the social structure cannot be separated from the state of the regional economy. They will be the ones most likely to be unskilled and tied by family responsibilities. If economic centralisation has particularly regressive effects, these women stand to gain very little.[23] Their only hope lies in certain aspects of the Social Charter, which is a set of policies designed to win wider support for the SEA by softening the worst effects of achieving the single market.

There are many aspects of the Social Charter of the Single European Act which will offer advances to working women, for example, the right to vocational training of every employee, the harmonisation of working conditions to move towards a common EC standard and special measures of support for disadvantaged groups in the workforce. There are proposals on childcare, parental leave and protection for part-time workers. However, these proposals are still at the discussion stage, and it will take a lot of hard campaigning before they become a reality. Moreover, the fact that these proposed directives have been consistently blocked by British ministers, using their powers of veto at the meetings of the Council of Ministers, does not augur well for the future. In December 1988 they blocked legislation on the burden of proof in sex discrimination cases, and previously they had blocked proposals on parental leave and childcare.

Conclusion

It is clear from the preceding analysis and discussion that women in Northern Ireland have come a long way over the past three decades. Their employment and occupational patterns have undergone significant change, determined primarily by industrial restructuring and the dominant role played by the public sector in the local economy. The decline of the traditional manufacturing industries means that the private sector has been replaced by the public sector as the main provider of female employment. High rates of male unemployment mean that Northern Ireland has one of the highest proportions of females in the employed labour force anywhere in the world. In fact 46% of total employees are women compared to 41% in Britain, 41% in the USA and 30% in the Irish Republic.[24]

There is evidence from the last Census of Population[25] that Catholic females are improving their position in the labour market significantly, relative to Catholic males. They have successfully entered some public-sector professions and groups of non-manual supervisory jobs. Certain groups of professional and non-manual women of both religions have succeeded in establishing equal status and pay levels with their male counterparts. Conversely, poorer women in manual occupations or dependent on state benefits are experiencing declining living standards and opportunities. In this sense they are truly in a place apart from their richer sisters. More than a decade of campaigning for equality has aided the upwardly mobile, without really touching the lives of women clustered in low-paying, undervalued occupations.

The impact of European economic integration is likely to exacerbate these divisions within peripheral regions like Northern Ireland. The benefits of 1992 seem likely to go to those European firms which can successfully link up with firms in other member states either through franchising, joint ventures or acquisition. The central Northern European economies will be at the hub of the activity while peripheries with no road or rail link to Europe will be fighting against tremendous odds. The major asset Northern Ireland will have in this situation will be its young, well-educated workforce, a large, if not the largest, proportion of which will be female.

As far as possibilities for women are concerned, there are signs of a welcome change ahead. Within the UK the impact of equal value legislation is beginning to reach down into the traditional female occupations, and the EOC is now targetting its activities exclusively on employment, training and childcare. At European level there are positive developments which are encouraging women, frustrated by ten years of campaigning in Thatcher's Britain, to look more favourably on Brussels and the possibilities it offers. Looking ahead into the 1990s, it is possible to predict better access to the fruits of equality campaigning for those groups previously excluded. If this does become a reality, new questions are immediately opened up concerning other dimensions of women's lives previously under-developed because of the struggle for economic independence and survival. For example, whether a larger share of bigger and better capitalist development is all that women want is questionable. There is a growing feeling that increased spending-power and consumption do not necessarily lead to happiness and contentment. An uncritical dependence on materialism, as well as raising levels of personal wealth, has brought in its wake increased indebtedness and irreparable damage to the environment. Women entered the male world and have found that it too has its negative aspects. Power seeking and competition are the hallmarks of business, and the need to adjust to these requirements is leading to unprecedented levels of stress, and stress-related illness in working women.

From a late twentieth-century perspective, the errors of unbridled growth are painfully apparent. It is the traditional female qualities of nurturing and caring which are the most offended by these threats of man-made catastrophe to the earth's atmosphere and climate. Environmental conditions affect everyone, men and women, rich and poor, all regions and all countries. There is no place apart. It is this growing awareness that is fostering new thinking about eradicating divisions between people and nations. It means looking at life in a deeper way, searching out the interdependencies, which can create the networks and relationships to express this need for balance and harmony, both within and without. To work towards this goal, as well as providing the economic systems to eradicate material want, is the challenge demanded by the future. If the 1990s bring more economic equality, women's sense of worth and value will move beyond the workplace. A maturing of women's concept of themselves and greater participation by women in all spheres of power and decision-making will enable a higher, more universal view to inform the issues. This will not, however, negate regional and national identities, which depend on distinctivness and integrity to make a specific case within federated structures. These shifting economic and ideological currents will affect women in Northern Ireland just as they are beginning to make an impact elsewhere. Closer links to Europe and a growing together of the island of Ireland after 1992 can only speed the process.

References

1. H. Morrissey, 'Unemployment and the Northern Ireland State 1919–1939', *The Other Crisis* (University of Ulster, 1984).
2. Employment statistics for Northern Ireland are collected on a quarterly basis by standard industrial classification and published by the Department of Economic Development, Netherleigh, Stormont, Belfast.
3. Equal Opportunities Commission (Northern Ireland), 'Woman-power no. 4' (Belfast, 1987).
4. R. J. Cormack and R. D. Osbourne, *Religion, Occupation and Employment 1971–1981*, (Belfast, Fair Employment Agency Northern Ireland, 1987).
5. The Census of Population 1981. Table produced from unpublished data by Cormack and Osbourne, note 4.
6. The Northern Ireland New Earnings Survey is published annually and is available from the Statistics Branch DED, Belfast.
7. Note 6.
8. Note 6.
9. R. Campbell, M. McWilliams and M. Morrissey, *A Review of the Gender Composition of Employment Patterns in Northern Ireland, with special reference to divisions of labour in the household economy.* (Belfast, EOC (Northern Ireland), 1989).
10. Regional Trends, 1988. Published on an annual basis by the Central Statistics Office, London. Available from HMSO.
11. Note 10.
12. Note 10.
13. Note 10.
14. A. Byrne, *Women and Poverty: A Review of the Statistics*, (University of Galway, 1988).
15. European Communities Commission, 'Women and Agriculture', *Women in Europe* (October 1988).

16. J. Blackwell, *Women in the Labour Force*, (Dublin, Employment Equality Agency, 1986).
17. Central Statistics Office (Dublin), 'Economic Series', (January 1989).
18. Progressive Democrats (Political Party), *Employment, Enterprise, and Tax Reform* (Dublin, 1988).
19. Northern Ireland New Earnings Survey, note 6.
20. M. Albert and R. Ball, *Towards European Economic Recovery in the 1980s* (Brussels, EC Commission, 1987).
21. Census of Employment 1986. DED Stormont. Export data supplied by the Northern Ireland Economic Council (Belfast).
22. Calculated from Northern Ireland Annual Abstract of Statistics. (Belfast, HMSO, 1988).
23. H. Morrissey, *Women in Ireland and the Impact of 1992*, (Belfast, Amalgamated Transport and General Workers Union, 1989).
24. Campbell, McWilliams and Morrissey, note 9.
25. Census of Population 1981, note 5.

8

Notes on the novel in Irish

Seán Hutton

As late as 1964, Breandán ó Doibhlin, novelist and critic, could write:

[Ní mór] don scríbhneoir Gaeilge . . . stíl do chruthú dó féin, foirm choincréideach focal do bhualadh ar a smaoineamh, foirm . . . atá ina toradh ar na céadta bliain de chultúr Eorpach agus a bhí á dealbhadh fiú i rith na tréimhse a raibh an Ghaeilge gan saothrú. Ní mór don Ghaeilge aistear chúig chéad bliain do dhéanamh agus éadáil gach tréimhse do bhailiú chuici in aimsir ghearr.[1]

[The writer in the Irish language . . . must create a style for himself, must impose a concrete form of words on his thoughts, a form . . . which is the result of hundreds of years of European cultural development and which was being moulded even during that period when Irish was not functioning as a literary language. Irish has to travel that five hundred years and has to gather to itself the riches of each period in a very short space of time.]

The Irish language had survived as, increasingly, a peasant language from the seventeenth century down to the end of the nineteenth century, the geographical area of its predominant use being progressively reduced, during a time when English was becoming the public language of the country, and the language associated with power and material success. There was a rich oral tradition and a poetic tradition which was represented increasingly in 'amhráin na ndaoine' [the songs of the people]. Few books were published in Irish, and classical and early modern

David Williams

texts survived in the hands of collectors and families (often belonging to the small-farming classes) with a tradition of learning.[2] However, there was little within the attenuated Gaelic prose tradition to which a writer of fiction might turn at the end of the nineteenth century, when what is regarded as the first example of the novel in the Irish language was published. This was *Séadna* by an tAthair [Father] Peadar ó Laoire, published in serial form in 1894 and in book form in 1904. This was a folknovel concerning a kindly shoemaker who is tricked into a pact with the devil (a different and more acceptable situation than that of Yeats's *Countess Cathleen*, who consciously sells her soul to save the people). One of the avowed purposes of its publication was '[to give] learners an opportunity and a means of becoming acquainted with . . . Irish syntax.'[3]

This connection between creative literature and the movement for the revival of the Irish language (initiated with the foundation of the Gaelic League in 1893) was to be a problematic one. To choose to write in Irish, a language in imminent danger of extinction, was in itself an act of commitment. Many were prepared to regard their writing as part of their effort 'ar son na cúise' [for The Cause]. The desperate need for reading matter with some contemporary bearing in the early years of this century meant that those who had a fluency in Irish, regardless of their creative ability, could far too easily establish a modest literary reputation and gain the kudos which went with it; and this established a pattern for the future. Further, the fact that the market which existed, and which expanded under the Irish Free State after 1922, was one which centred on school children and adult learners meant that, for example, a major Irish language writer like Pádraig ó Conaire felt, in the 1920s, that he was diverted from his main task to the production of trivia in an attempt to earn a living. Another major writer, Seosamh Mac Grianna, experienced a similar alienation in the 1930s. Few could live the contradictions as successfully as Máirtín ó Cadhain, a writer of superbly imaginative fiction, a school- and, later, university-teacher, a sometimes acerbic critic, and a pugnacious campaigner on behalf of the Irish language. But he was conscious of those contradictions and their effects:

> Tá rud níos measa ná an t-uireasa aitheantais sa mbaile agus i gcéin ag goilliúint ar an scríbhneoir. Is deacair do dhuine a dhícheall a dhéanamh i dteanga arb é a cosúlacht go mbeidh

sí básaithe roimhe féin. . . . Fonn troda go fíochmhar ar a son a ghineas an t-éadóchas sin ann. Ní go maith dhó mar scríbhneoir atá an t-éadóchas ná an troid. An rud is marfaí faoin troid seo gur ag caidreamh le 'lucht na cúise', an dream is beagmhaitheasaí in Éirinn agus cuid acu is claoine freisin, a thairraingeos sí e.[4]

[There is something troubling the writer which is worse than the lack of recognition at home and abroad. It is difficult for a person to perform at his best in a language which will quite likely be dead before him. . . . A desire to fight fiercely on its behalf is the reaction that despair provokes. Despair and campaigning are not good for the writer. And the most terrible thing about this campaigning is that it draws him into contact with the supporters of The Cause, the most useless group of people in Ireland and, some of them, the crookedest.]

With the revival of prose fiction in Irish at the turn of the present century, debate turned on whether this should be true to a specific Irish (folk) tradition or whether it should have a wider perspective. P. H. Pearse, the writer, educationalist and Irish separatist, who was a leading exponent of the latter view, argued that

> We must get into touch . . . with our contemporaries – in France, in Russia, in Norway . . . wherever, in short, vital literature is being produced on the face of the globe. . . . Irish literature, if it is to live and grow, must get into contact on the one hand with its own past and on the other with the mind of contemporary Europe.[5]

On the other hand, the prolific short story writer and novelist 'Máire' [Mary] (Séamus ó Grianna – 'as popular as a writer in Irish can be and the most prolific novelist to date in Irish'[6]), was one of those who felt strongly that there was a specific Irish mode:

> Bhí *art* daobhtha féin ag seanchuidhthibh Gaedhilge. Bhí dóigh náisiúnta aca leis an sgéal a innse. D'fhás an t-*art* sin amach as saoghal agus as creideamh na ndaoine. Ní hionann ár saoghal féin agus ceann na Sasana nó na Fraince. . . . Ba cheart cruth an tsean-sgéil a choinneáil beo agus *art* Gaedh-lach a shníomh amach as. Deirtear linn go gcoinneochadh seo ar gcúl litridheacht na Gaedhilge. . . . Ach shílfinn go bhfuil sé contabhairteach a cur ar chosaibh anáirde agus an

codladh ina súilibh. B'fhéidir gur síos i súmaire a thuitfeadh
sí leis an deifre.[7]

[The Irish seannnachies had an art of their own. They had a
national way of telling a story. That art developed out of the
life and the belief of the people. Our life is not the life of
England or France. . . . We should keep the form of the old
story alive and develop from it an Irish art. We are told that
this will retard literature in Irish. . . . But I believe that it is
wrong to set off at a gallop with sleep still in the eyes. There is
the danger of being sucked down, into a quagmire in one's
haste.]

Terence Brown in chapters 1 and 2 of *Ireland: A Social and Cultural
History 1922–79*, provides a succinct account of the background
against which literary production in Irish and English took place
in the Irish Free State after 1922. The composition of the alliance
which upheld and reproduced the values of the Irish state down
to the 1960s is described as follows:

> The combined force of . . . the farmers and the tradesmen,
> together with such of their offspring as could find roles in the
> professions was enormously influential in fashioning the
> political, social and cultural moulds of the independent
> state. Their economic prudence, their necessarily puri-
> tanical, repressive sexual mores and nationalistic conserva-
> tism, encouraged by a priesthood and Hierarchy drawn
> considerably from their number, largely determined the
> kind of country which emerged in the first decades of
> independence.[8]

This alliance – which had been already colonising the institutions
of the British state in Ireland in the nationalist areas in the
pre-independence period – represented the agency through
which the ideologies of secular and cultural nationalism, pro-
pounded by national figures (like Parnell, Redmond, MacNeill,
Hyde and Pearse) were filtered and assimilated to more traditional patterns of thought.

In *An Litríocht Réigiúnach* [Regional Literature], Máirín Nic Eoin
examines the ideological underpinnings of modern writing in
Irish in the first half of this century. She rightly attaches great
importance to the ideology of the Gaelic League, which was
based on an idealised image of the people of the Gaeltacht as the
repositories of the Irish language and the oral tradition. This

ideology came to dominate the language and Gaelic literary movements and was integrated into the dominant ideology of the Irish state.[9] 'People's history' has a strong resonance within Irish populist-nationalist ideology; and the elevating of the import-ance of peasant autobiography – plus the success of a number of examples of the form in Ireland and outside – encouraged emulation and influenced the development of prose writing in Irish. Of the eight twentieth-century prose works chosen by John Jordan for his radio series, 'The Pleasures of Gaelic Literature', broadcast by Radio Éireann in the 1970s, three were straight-forward autobiographies, one was a fictionalised autobiography, one was a satire on the genre, and only two were novels.[10] The importance attached to the peasantry has influenced the whole question of language as well as form:

> Ba ar an gcaint sna saothair liteartha is mó a bhí aird na léirmheastóirí dírithe. . . . Moladh leabhair ar son na dea-Ghaeilge a bhí le fáil iontu nó ar son an léiriú fírinneach a bhí le feicéail iontu ar aigne na nGael.[11]

> [Reviewers directed their attention chiefly to the language of the work. . . . Books were praised for the fine quality of the Irish to be found in them or on account of the accuracy of their representation of the Irish mind.]

An interesting recent example of this occurs in the 1983 reprint of 'Máire's' *Tairngreacht Mhiseoige* [Miseog's Prophecy] (1958). In a cover-note, it is recognised that the romantic style of the book is out of fashion at the present time, but it is felt that readers will still enjoy 'an stíl éasca agus an teanga shaibhir' [the fluent style and the rich language] of the book. (Of course the acceptable version of the Irish peasantry was a sanitised version, as events as diverse as the 'Playboy' riots at the Abbey Theatre in 1907 and the events which followed the publication of *The Tailor and Ansty* by Eric Cross in 1942, illustrate.[12]) In many ways literary effort was viewed from the perspective of its role in the consolidation of the language and that problematic entity, the nation.[13] This, though, is hardly surprising when we keep in mind the vast effort of mobilisation which had been accomplished around the issues of Home Rule and national independence at the end of the nineteenth and the beginning of the twentieth centuries.

The wide range of mainstream authors translated into Irish through the scheme initiated by An Gúm [The Plan] after 1926 (they include Wells, Scott, Dickens, Conan Doyle, Chesterton,

Stevenson, Conrad, Turgenev, Ibsen, Jules Verne, Dumas, Jerome K. Jerome, William Carleton, Charles Kickham, George Birmingham and Shan Bullock) suggests that if writers in Irish were not reading adventurously, they were at least in some form of communication with a wider literary world, if only for the purpose of earning the fee per thousand words for translations. While they more or less unconsciously absorbed various dominant ideas about literary production, the majority of Gaelic prose writers gave little thought to literary theory or aesthetics. The model which influenced the average writer was the romantic novelette or the adventure story.[14] Seán ó Tuama gives examples of the plots of two typical novels, *Ceol na nGiolcach* by Pádraig óg ó Conaire and *Caisleán Óir* by 'Máire':

> . . . ins gach ceann den dá leabhar tá laoch agus banlaoch atá chomh glan geanmnaí leis an sneachta séite agus a bhfuil grá buan maoithneach acu dá chéile; is beirt iad nach eol dóibh aon éagóir, cé go ndéantar éagóirí orthu – beirt nach bhfuil a macasamhail ar dhroim an domhain![15]

> [in each of the two books there is a hero and a heroine who are as pure as the driven snow and who love each other with a lasting, sentimental love; they are a pair who know no evil, although they are the victims of evil – they are a pair whose like does not exist on the face of the earth!]

The novel in Irish, down to the 1960s, came a poor second in terms of frequency of production, to other literary forms. This has certainly been due to the fact that periodicals represented one of the most probable avenues for publication; and here the poem, the short story or the essay was more likely to achieve publication. That, almost without exception, writers in Irish were part-time writers, many being teachers or civil servants, has also infuenced literary form in a way which has militated against the novel.[16] Certainly one of the most remarkable achievements of this literary revival has been the development of poetry in Irish since ó Direáin and ó Ríordáin led the way in the 1940s and 1950s. Here again the achievement has been in the area of the miniature – what Máirtín ó Cadhain described dismissively as '[an] liric dheas neamhurchóideach' [the pretty, harmless, lyric].[17] The writer of both novels and short stories in Irish working within the the canons of social realism – which Máirín Nic Eoin identifies as a dominant form within creative writing in Irish[18] – is faced with the problem of creating a credible world picture through the medium of a language which is a means of social communication (in the full sense) only in the rural Gaeltachtaí. It was strongly put to me a few years ago by Máirtín ó Direáin, a poet and essayist who had thought deeply about questions of literary form, that this latter fact concerning the Irish language made its use impossible in treating of urban/modern experience successfully in prose fiction, especially in the form of the novel. He did admit, when pressed, however, that there were stylistic strategies – the interior monologue, for example – through which this perceived difficulty could be overcome. Máirtín ó Cadhain, in fact, went to the heart of the matter when he wrote:

> . . . ní hí fírinne na cumadóireacht, na healaíne, fírinne an tsaoil. . . . Ní cóir iarra ar úrscéal ar bith a bheith inchreidthe ach de réir a chuid téarmaí tagartha. . . . I scéal áirid . . . chuir mise i gcás gur thosaigh tithe i mbaile mór áirid ag buala faoin a chéile. D'fhéach mé le chuile shórt eile a dhéanamh inchreidthe taobh istigh den fhráma sin.[19]

> [the truth of creative literature, of art, is not the truth of life. . . . One cannot ask that any novel should be believable except within its own terms of reference . . . In a certain story. . . . I started from the supposition that the houses in a certain town had begun to knock against each other. I sought to make all the rest believable within that context.]

It is, however, true that the particular history of the Irish language has given a unique importance to questions of language and form. The issues to be faced in these areas are different from those besetting the writer of English in Ireland, and from the 1960s onwards prose writers in Irish began to address them, as will become clear.

In 1926 An Gúm was set up, under the control, significantly, of the Department of Education, to supervise the publication of books in Irish. Until the setting up of An Gúm, publication of Irish texts was carried out by the Gaelic League and a small number of private publishers. 'Máire', in his autobiography *Saol Corrach* [Troubled Times], poured scorn on the operation An Gúm, especially its policy of commissioning translations of works from other languages into Irish at a pound per thousand words.[20] The contempt of such writers for An Gúm has fixed an image in the minds of the Irish-speaking public towards it which persists. There is no doubt that its objective of publishing works for schoolchildren and learners of Irish, combined with the bureaucratic and puritanical outlook of the civil servants who controlled it, meant that much work of no literary merit was published, and that worthwhile works remained unpublished or on the stocks for years.[21] However, there is need for a detailed study of An Gúm in the broader context of the attempts of an emerging state to create a specific national identity for itself, and interesting comparative work could be done here.

Máirín Nic Eoin, as already mentioned, has pointed to social realism as a dominant form.[22] She states, in explanation:

> Baineann sé seo leis an gcaoi a n-úsáideann scríbhneoirí áirithe Gaeilge an t-úrscéal mar iompróir teachtaireachta sóisialta nuair ba chuí agus nuair ab fheiliúnaí an t-ábhar atá faoi chaibidil a phlé ar bhealach eile ar fad – i dtráchtas, in alt nó i leabhar taighde, mar shampla.[23]

> [This is related to the way in which certain writers in Irish use the novel to convey a social message when it would be more appropriate to present the subject in question in a totally different manner – as a thesis, or as an article or as a work of reference, for example.]

This didactic tendency has been a persistent one, and Breandán ó Doibhlin, a champion of an Irish form of modernism, could write, in the preface to his novel, *Néal Maidine agus Tine Oíche* (a book of which it is said in a cover-note, 'Féachann an leabhar le roinnt dár gcuid fadhbanna cultúrtha a scagadh trí mhachnamh i modh siombalach a dhéanamh orthu' [The book seeks to examine some of our cultural problems by reflecting on them using a language of symbols]): 'Dá scríobhfainnse leabhar fealsúnachta, lán de chruthúnais agus de chonclúidí agus de dheifnidí, níor thógtha ort dá mb'hearr leat gan tabhairt faoina léamh.'[24] [If I were to write a philosophical treatise, full of proofs and conclusions and definitions, you could not be blamed for not wishing to read it.]

In the period from the 1890s onwards, much of the groundwork which created the conditions for the revival of literature in Irish was laid. Basic teaching materials were published, the earlier literature and folklore were made accessible to the modern, non-academic reader, and Irish-language teaching was established within the education system. The setting-up of the Irish Free State in 1922 assisted this process. The attempt to achieve much quickly, and on too narrow a front – laying the weight of the revival effort on the primary schools – meant that problems were created for the future. In the meantime, while the number of native Irish-speakers (those who spoke Irish as their first language) continued to decline, outside the Gaeltacht the number of people who defined themselves as having a competency in the Irish language increased.[25] By the mid-century a number of the problems which Cahalan identified as facing Irish writers had been removed or substantially mitigated: 'the lack of any clearly fixed language to write in, the absence of a tradition or a community of writers, and the fact that even if the writer somehow did manage to write, there would be no publishers to disseminate the writing and no reading public to read it.'[26] Adoption by An Club Leabhar (after 1948) could secure a readership of up to 3000 for a book in Irish.[27] If this seems, as it is, a very restricted readership, there are compensations for the writer in a small, intimate society like that of Ireland, as is clear from the following passage written by Máirtín ó Cadhain:

> Tá a fhios agam gur thug an gnáthphobal, thiar ar aon nós, agus seo iad mo mhuintir féin, an-taithneamh do *Chré na Cille*. Cheannaigh daoine san áit sin í nár cheannaigh de leabhar ariamh ach *Old Moore's Almanac* . . ., nó an *Imeldist* ó na mná rialta nuair nach raibh aon dul as acu . . . bhíodh sí dhá léamh sna tithe cuart agus ar an bportach. . . . Agus bhí pobal eile ann. Is mór an rud ag scríbhneoir aitheantas. É seo a chloisteáil ag dul thart dhom i bPáirc an Chrócaigh lá mórchluiche: 'there goes Cré na Cille'.[28]

> [I know that the ordinary people, in the west anyway – and those are my own people – got great enjoyment from *Cré na Cille*. People bought it in places where the only book purchased previously was *Old Moore's Almanac* . . . or the *Imeldist* from the nuns if there was no way of avoiding a purchase . . . it was read in the houses where people gathered at night and out on the turf bogs. . . . And there was another public as well. Recognition is an important thing for the writer. To overhear this, one day when I was at a big match in Croke Park: 'there goes Cré na Cille'.]

The improvement in the situation of the writer in Irish in the period during and after the Second World War can be indicated by the following chronology:

1939 Foundation of Cumann na Scríbhneoirí (Writers Association)

1939 Revival of Oireachtas literary competitions
1942 Foundation of the magazine *Comhar*
1943 Foundation of newspaper *Inniu*
1945 Foundation of publishing house Sáirséal agus Dill
1948 Foundation of magazine *Feasta*
1948 Foundation of An Club Leabhar (the Book Club)
1952 Government scheme to give financial assistance for the
      publication of books in Irish by private publishers.[29]

This period, from the late 1930s onwards, was also a period
which saw the publication of a number of landmarks in the
'nualitríocht' [modern literature]: Máirtín ó Direáin's first four
volumes of poetry between 1942 and 1947, Seán ó Ríordáin's
collection *Eireaball Spideoige* [The Robin's Tail] (1952), Seosamh
Mac Grianna's *Mo Bhealach Féin* [My Own Way] (1940), Myles na
gCopaleen's *An Béal Bocht* [The Poor Mouth] (1941), and Máirtín ó
Cadhain's *Cré na Cille* [The Clay of the Grave] (1949). These three
prose works, with Pádraig ó Conaire's expressionist novel
Deoraíocht [Exile] (1910), are among a handful of recognisably
modern works produced during the first half-century of the
Gaelic literary revival. James M. Cahalan describes *Deoraíocht* (a
work which An tAthair Peadar ó Laoire attempted to have
removed from the Irish course for matriculation to the National
University in 1917 on grounds of immorality) as 'the most
innovative, forward-looking Irish novel in either language
during this period before the arrival of Joyce as a novelist'.[30] All go
against the grain of the dominant ideology of the revival and
literary movements. The narrator of *Mo Bhealach Féin* is a
profoundly alienated outsider.[31] *An Béal Bocht* is a satire on the
revivalists' romanticisation of the Irish-speaking peasant and the
literary and other conventions which followed from this.[32] The
savage jealousies and hatreds of the dead in the graveyard of *Cré
na Cille* – a novel which consists almost exclusively of dialogue –
marks the protagonists as far removed from the cotton-wool
heroes and heroines of run-of-the-mill revivalist fiction from the
moment Caitríona Pháidín utters the famous opening words of
the book: 'Ní mé an ar Áit an Phuint nó na Cúig Déag atá mé
curtha?' [I wonder if I'm buried in the Pound Plot or the
Fifteen-Shilling Plot?][33]

The 1960s was a period when the consensus and the stifling
conservatism which had arisen in Ireland during the early 1920s
was beginning to break down. There was a greater willingness,

on a wider scale, to consider new possibilites. The unemployment and the heavy emigration of the 1950s added to that
awareness, which already existed among some intellectuals and
political dissidents, that the ideology which had characterised the
movement to independence had a hollow ring to it. At the same
time the outside world was beginning to impinge more generally
on Ireland, a process which was aided greatly by the advent of
television. Máirín Nic Eoin detects a change from the 1960s
onwards with regard to writing in Irish:

> . . . ní hamháin go bhfuil méadú substaintiúil tagtha ar líon
> na n-úrscéalta ach tosaíodh freisin ar bhealaí nua a thriail,
> ábhair agus timpeallachtaí nua a léiriú agus a phlé, foir-
> meacha turgnamhacha a thástáil agus fealsúnachtaí liteartha
> éagsúla a fhorbairt agus a chraoladh trí mheán na húrscéa-
> laíochta Gaeilge.[34]

> [. . . not only was there a substantial increase in the number
> of novels produced, but a beginning was made also in trying
> out new styles; new subjects and environments were dealt
> with; experimental forms were tried out and various literary
> philosophies were developed and made familiar through the
> novel in Irish.]

This widening of literary horizons has certainly been assisted by
the gradual evolution of more satisfactory standards of criticism
in Irish. Among the pioneers here were the author Eoghan ó
Tuairisc and the group of people around *Irisleabhar Mhá Nuad*,
which included, and includes, an tAthair Breandán ó Doibhlin.[35]
The burgeoning of the novel and the expansion of creative
writing in general must have owed something also to the
willingness of enterprising publishers to take on and publish
work. Seosamh Mac Grainna's *An Druma Mór*, which was written
in 1929–30, was not published by An Gúm until 1969, by which
time its author had ceased to write altogether, had suffered a
complete breakdown and had become institutionalised. Máirtín ó
Cadhain had been told that An Gúm would not publish his
'gáirsiúlacht' [filth], when Sáirseál agus Dill undertook to publish
his masterpiece, *Cré na Cille*.[36] The high literary standard of
Comhar and *Feasta*, exposure through these and other periodicals
and through paperback translations in English to modern European literature, plus the possibility of Oireachtas awards and
access to a relatively wide audience through An Club Leabhar,
must also have helped.

Novels like an tAthair Breandán ó Doibhlin's *Néal Maidine agus Tine Oíche* [Morning Cloud and Night Fire] (1964), Eoghan ó Tuairisc's *Dé Luain* [Monday] (1966) and Diarmaid ó Suailleabháin's *Caoin Tú Féin* [Lament Your Fate] (1967) are examples of this development from writers who, very importantly, came from outside the Gaeltacht and to whom Irish was an acquired, second language. Significantly, in view of doubts about the national destiny, *Néal Maidine agus Tine Oíche* is a political allegory concerning the odyssey of a chosen people revealed in the reflections of a chosen leader. Equally significant, in view of the primacy attached to the spoken Irish of the people in revivalist ideology, and by writers like 'Máire', is the use of a highly literary language, far removed from 'caint na ndaoine' [the speech of the people] – though here, as so often elsewhere, one must register Máirtín ó Cadhain's influence on younger writers and his dictum concerning 'Dinneen's Dictionary' '[gur] chóir do chuile scríbhneoir i a thabhairt chun leapan leis' [which every writer should take to bed with him].[37] *Dé Luain*, a fine historical novel concerning the 1916 Rising, uses a cinematic technique to give a kaleidoscopic picture of events and motivations. Speaking of the composition of *Dé Luain*, ó Tuairisc said,

> Bíonn rudaí áirithe ag baint le Gaeilge de bhrí nach raibh an Ghaeilge in sáid le 300 bliain nó mar sin . . . an chéad rúd a bhí le déanamh agam ná foclóir a dhéanamh amach dom féin as fréamhacha na Gaeilge . . . sa chás seo, sa litríocht . . . Baineann sé sin le Gaeilge. . . . Ní fíor é maidir le teangacha eile. Is féidir leat cur síos ar thréimhse ar bith sa Bhéarla, tá foclóir chomh leathan sin agat. . . .[38]

> [Irish has certain characteristics arising from the fact that it was not in use for 300 years or so . . . the first thing I had to do was to make myself a dictionary from the root-stock of Irish . . . in this case, literature. . . . That's something that pertains to Irish . . . It isn't true with regard to other languages. You can write about any period in English, you have such a wide vocabulary. . . .]

In *Caoin Tú Féin*, the narrator, coming out of an almighty hangover, attempts to come to terms with the collapse of his personal life. Objects and events are registered in the mind of the subject of the novel and the style mirrors his attempt to pull the fragments into some coherent shape. Also significant is Eoghan ó Tuairisc's *An Lomnochtáin* [The Naked One] (1977), where the author seeks to develop a language and a style to describe the expanding world-picture of a young boy growing-up in the English-speaking midlands of Ireland, using a stream-of-consciousness technique.

A preoccupation with language and style is, not unnaturally in the circumstances, a characteristic of many writers since the l960s.[39] Of Alan Titley's novel *Méirscrí na Treibhe* [A Split within the Tribe] (1978), Máirín Nic Eoin remarks,

> Is sa leabhar seo, thar aon áit eile, a chomhlíonarn Alan Titley a fhealsúnacht liteartha féin – gurb í an teanga agus caidreamh an údair léi an rud is tábhachtaí, an rud a dhéanann saothar fiúntach de leabhar. . . . Is í an teanga féin atá ag gníomhú anseo, dár dtimpeallú, dár dtachtadh, dár ndalladh.[40]
>
> [It is in this book especially that Alan Titley gives effect to his literary philosophy – that it is language and the author's engagement with it that is most important, that it is this which transforms a work of fiction into a worthwhile product. . . . It is language itself which is at work here surrounding us, choking us, blinding us.]

Mícheál ó Brolacháin, author of the bleak post-holocaust *Pax Dei* (1985), is concerned with the development of a language which will reflect the strongly accented and slangy 'Gaeilge bhriste' [broken Irish] of the young Dublin Irish speaker. Séamus Mac Annaidh, author of *Cuaifeach mo Londubh Buí* [The Tempest of My Yellow/Orange Blackbird] (1983) and *Mo Dhá Mhicí* [My Two Mickeys] (1986), shows a similar preoccupation with language. Parts of both novels (which form volumes one and two of a trilogy) are written in mixtures of Irish and English, and in the *Cuaifeach* one of the characters refuses altogether to speak Irish. In both books, though more particularly in the *Cuaifeach*, there are outrageous puns, subversions of literary references, bendings of language, ambiguities, multiple meanings; and the author is, in both, as visible as Laurence Sterne (in *Tristram Shandy*) or Jean Genet. The boundaries between author/text/reader are constantly assaulted: for example, by the refrain which is repeated throughout the *Cuaifeach*, 'Is cuma faoin scéal. Amharc sna súile agam. Déanaimis caidreamh.' [The story doesn't matter. Look into ny eyes. Let's get it together.], which reminds one of those Renaissance paintings where the subject of the painting appears to be extending a foot or a hand outside the frame into the space of the observer; or again, in *Mo Dhá Mhící*, by the invitation to the reader to participate in painting a number of word pictures which form a background to, or gloss on, the events of the novel – 'Léitheoireacht chruthaitheach'[41] [creative/active reading] indeed! The *Cuaifeach* is a complex work in which time, personality and personal identity attain a bewildering fluidity, while a number of the central characters are obsessed with the desire for immortality.[42]

Mac Annaidh has described his first novel as a '*Punk*-leabhair' [punk-book].[43] The title of his second novel is a play on the title of 'Maire's' first novel, *Mo Dhá Róisín* [My Two Róisíns] (1921). Labhras óg [Young Larry] has two loves, a woman and Ireland. Although in love with him, brown-haired Róisín has vowed that she will not marry until Ireland (Dark Róisín) is free. He fights in the Easter Rising and lays down his life for his two Róisíns. We meet brown-haired Róisín at the conclusion of the book, still lamenting his death. Mac Annaidh's *Mo Dhá Mhící* is in many respects a subversion of 'Máire's' work, informed by the questioning spirit of 'Máire's' brother, the writer Seosamh Mac Grianna. The Blackbirdness propagated by Micí Mac Crosáin ('Mr Blackbird') is a sort of divine, anarchic madness seeking an openness which would transcend the sectarian/political divisions in Northern Ireland. One of its antitheses in the novel is represented by Justine Nic Anna, the tight-lipped, puritanical and sexually frustrated teacher, who is portrayed as blindly and bigotedly nationalist. However, its episodic anti-linear structure, its many ambiguities, its lack a conventional conclusion make it anything but a didactic work. 'Ariel', the Protestant schoolboy, is the agent whom Micí (Prospero) would use as the catalyst in the plot which never develops.

Mac Annaidh is one of the most challenging of the contemporary Irish-language novelists. His choice of the Irish language places him in the context of preoccupations which are island-wide. Nevertheless, his second novel is very much a book out of Northern Ireland today. Referring to the writing of poetry in Irish in Northern Ireland, Greagóir ó Dúill states, 'Continuing political problems . . . have created a situation where few of the most published poets are apolitical and all are, to some extent, didactic'. James Hawthorn, the chairman of the new Cultural Traditions Group, which has been recently set up in Northern Ireland, has been quoted as saying, 'Scanraíonn an Ghaeilge naonur as deichniúr den mhuintir lena bhainimse' – adding 'ach níl mise ina measc siúd' [Nine out of ten people in my community are frightened by Irish . . . though that's not true in my case].[44] This means that the Irish language is, in effect, the language with which the nationalist minority identifies. While the Irish language is recognised within the school system, and, while under the new Cultural Heritage programme, its historic importance will be recognised[45], one could hardly say that it has been encouraged in the past by the Northern Ireland state. While Protestant-unionist individuals have taken an interest in the Irish language intermittently, the fact that campaigns around the language are essentially nationalist-republican campaigns, makes Irish a political issue in a rather different way than in the Republic of Ireland. Here there is still a broad consensus that in some sense the Irish language is a national issue.[46] In Northern Ireland, in reality, Irish has been seen as a nationalist community issue up to the present. It is not strange then that there is less space for the writer in Irish than for the writer in English. Mac Annaidh, who reacts against the pressures which the politics of the language places on the writer, creates that cultural space in his own work, though that work is sufficiently complex to reflect the constraints which restrict that space in reality. Mac Annaidh is fighting to create the space which writers in the Republic of Ireland created in the post-independence period in rather different circumstances. He is attempting something important in *Mo Dhá Mhicí* which sets-up a dialectic between vision and reality.

The propaganda and educational work of the Gaelic League and the establishment of an Irish state at the beginning of the twentieth century, together with the education programmes of successive Irish governments, all contributed to the creation of conditions under which Irish prose literature could be revived. The period under consideration has been one in which the considerable work of catching up, which Breandán ó Doibhlin described as necessary, has been accomplished, especially since the 1960s. If the myths created in the process of state-building have had to be challenged, and if the policies of the state have been less than adequate in the eyes of many revivalists, the disillusionment and demystification which has accompanied some sixty years of political independence in the Republic of Ireland have in their way, contributed to the maturity of prose writing in Irish, much of the best of which has been written 'against the grain'. The development of a modern literature in Irish has also been dependent, as the modernisers hoped and felt it should have been, on an increasing awareness of developments in modern Hiberno-English literature and in literature outside Ireland. That this has been accomplished in a small island on the margin of Europe, in a language which is being shored-up against decline, in a century when the power of supra-national mass communications has been incessantly increasing, may in the fulness of non-Celtic time come to be regarded as a variation on the theme:

> Do not go gentle into that good night,
> Rage, rage against the dying of the light.

However, that will be for posterity to judge. It is for writers in Irish, in the meantime, to proceed with their task of gracing and enhancing an ancient language through encounters of imagination and reality.

Note: Perceptive readers of this essay will have noted that Irish writers, like so many others, have written with the grammatical assumption that the writer is inevitably 'he'. This convention has been retained in translations from the Irish in the text. Readers will also have noted that all the prose writers referred to are men. The absence of women prose writers in the Irish language, outside autobiography, is a notable phenomenon. Since the 1960s women have been emerging as poets and critics – Máire Mhac an tSaoi is a notable figure from a previous generation. However, there is still a lack of women prose writers. The whole political economy of the family and the home resting on a sexual division of labour (labour including in this sense housework and child-rearing), has no doubt contributed greatly to this phenomenon, just as it has elsewhere; so that the woman's main contribution to literature in Irish has probably been in the area of logistic support, and, increasingly in the post-1960s, in terms of contribution to domestic income which has enabled men to 'find the time' to write. The social and ideolgical background of many writers in Irish, which reinforced traditional assumptions, may also be relevant here.

References

1. Breandán ó Doibhlin, *Néal Maidine agus Tine Oíche* (Dublin, Foil-seacháin Náisiúnta Teoranta, 1964), p. 11.
2. Maureen Wall, 'The Decline of the Irish Language', in Brian ó Cuív, ed., *A View of the Irish Language* (Dublin, Stationery Office, 1969), pp. 81–90; Gearóid ó Tuathaigh, *Ireland Before the Famine* (Dublin, Gill

and Macmillan, 1972), pp. 157–9; Tomás ó Concheanainn, ed., *Nua-Dhuanaire 111* (Dublin, Institúid an Ardléinn, 1978); Breandán ó Conchúir, *Scríobhaithe Chorcaí, 1700–1850* (Dublin, An Clóchomhar, 1982).

3. James M. Cahalan, *The Irish Novel* (Dublin, Gill and Macmillan, 1988), p. 115; Máirtín ó Cadhain, *Páipéir Bhána agus Páipéir Bhreacha* (Dublin, An Clóchomhar, 1969), p. 19; Seán ó Tuama, 'Úrscéalta agus Faisnéisí Beatha na Gaeilge: Na Buaicphointí', in Seán ó Mórdha, ed., *Scríobh 5* (Dublin, An Clóchomhar, 1981), p. 148. A version of Seán ó Tuama's article is published in Patrick Rafroidi and Maurice Harmon, eds., *The Irish Novel in Our Time* (Lille, Lille University Press, 1976).

4. ó Cadhain, note 3, p. 40.

5. Quoted in Cahalan, note 3, p. 116.

6. Cahalan, note 3, p. 184.

7. Quoted in Nollaig Mac Congáil, *Scríbhneoirí Thír Chonaill* (Dublin, Foilseacháin Náisiúnta Teoranta, 1983), p. 23.

8. Terence Brown, *Ireland: A Social and Cultural History l922–1979* (London, Fontana, 1981), p. 26.

9. Máirín Nic Eoin, *An Litríocht Réigiúnach* (Dublin, An Clochómhar, 1982), pp. 15, 16–17, 23.

10. Nic Eoin, note 9, pp. 33–41; John Jordan, ed., *The Pleasures of Gaelic Literature* (Cork, Mercier, 1977).

11. Nic Eoin, note 9, p. 49.

12. See Frank O'Connor's introduction to Eric Cross, *The Tailor and Ansty* (Cork, Mercier Press, 1985), pp. 5–9.

13. Nic Eoin, note 9, pp. 24–7.

14. ó Tuama, note 3, p. 151.

15. ó Tuama, note 3, p. 151.

16. Nic Eoin, note 3, p. 27; Máirín Nic Eoin, 'Úrscéalaíocht na Gaeilge 1974–1984', *Comhar* (August 1984), 15.

17. ó Cadhain, note 3, p. 37.

18. Nic Eoin, note 16, p. 16.

19. ó Cadhain, note 3, pp. 10, 12. On this whole issue of realism and literary style, see Louis de Paor's discussion of the contrasting styles of *Súil le Breith* by Pádraig Standún and *Cuaifeach mo Londubh Bui* by Séamas Mac Annaidh in 'Mo Dhá Lon Dubh', *Comhar*, (December 1987), 12–16.

20. Séamus ó Grianna, *Saol Corrach* (Cork, Mercier, 1981), pp. 234–240.

21. ó Tuama, note 3, p. 152; ó Cadhain (note 3), p. 28; Gearóid S Mac Eoin, 'Twentieth Century Irish Literature', in ó Cuív, ed., note 2, p. 62; Nic Eoin, note 3, pp. 28–30. An interesting examination of one writer's interaction with An Gúm is contained in Maolmhaodhóg ó Ruairc, 'Seosamh Mac Grianna: Aistritheoir', *Comhar*, (January 1988), 30–4.

22. Nic Eoin, note 16, p. 16.

23. Nic Eoin, note 16, p. 16.
24. ó Doibhlin, note 1, p. 13.
25. Proinsias ó Conluain and Donncha ó Céileachair, *An Duinníneach*, (Dublin, Sáirséal and Dill, 1958), pp. 214–15; Brown (note 8), pp. 51–63; Aindrias ó Muimhneacháin, *Dóchas agus Duainéis: Scéal Chonradh na Gaeilge 1922–1932* (Cork, Mercier, n.d.), pp. 17–23, 77–96.
26. Cahalan, note 3, p. 113.
27. ó Tuama, note 3, p. 157.
28. ó Cadhain, note 3, p. 13.
29. Mac Eoin, note 21, p. 64; ó Tuama, note 3, p. 157; Máirín Ní Mhuiríosa, 'Cumann na Scríbhneoirí : Memoir', in Seán ó Mórdha, ed., note 3, p. 168; Eibhlín Ní Chathailriabhaigh, 'An tOireachtas 1939–1988', *Feasta*, (October 1988), 80.
30. Cahalan, note 3, p. 117. On An tAthair Peadar and *Deoraíocht* see, Tomás de Bhaldraithe, ed., *Pádraic ó Conaire: Clocha ar a Charn* (Dublin, An Clóchomhar, 1982), pp. 101–6.
31. Liam ó Dochartaigh, '*Mo Bhealach Féin*: Saothar Nualitríochta', in Seán ó Mórdha, ed., note 3, p. 240.
32. Cahalan, note 3, pp. 243–245.
33. Cahalan, note 3, pp. 253–257.
34. Nic Eoin, note 16, p. 15. However, traditional novels did continue to be produced. Pádraig Standún's *Súil le Breith* [Expecting] (1983) and Dónall Mac Amhlaigh's *Deoraithe* [Exiles] (1986) are successful examples.
35. Nic Eoin, note 16, p. 16.
36. Niall ó Dónaill, 'Cuimhne Phearsanta', *Comhar*, (January 1988), 25; Liam ó Dochartaigh, 'Scéalaí Chúige Uladh: Spléachadh ar Scéalta Staire Sheosaimh Mhic Grianna', *Comhar*, (January 1988), 40; ó Cadhain, note 3, p. 28.
37. ó Cadhain, note 3, p. 17.
38. 'Fornocht . . . Comhrá le hEoghan ó Tuairisc', *Innti*, 6, 28.
39. On the novel in Irish since the 1960s see Nic Eoin, note 16, p. 15; Cahalan (note 3), pp. 281–285; ó Tuama, note 3, pp. 157–8.
40. Nic Eoin, note 16, p. 19.
41. ó Doibhlin, note 1, p. 13.
42. On Mac Annaidh's novels see Micheál Mac Craith, 'Ag cur rudaí as a riocht ar mhaithe le héifeacht', *Comhar*, (December 1987), 44–51.
43. 'Comhar-Rá 10', *Comhar*, (August 1984), 25.
44. Greagóir ó Dúill, 'Ulster Poetry in Irish', *Poetry Ireland Review*, 25, 82–3; 'Tuarascáil', *Irish Times*, (12 July 1989).
45. See *Cultural Heritage: A Cross Curricular Theme–Report of the Cross Curricular Working Group on Cultural Heritage to the Parliamentary Under Secretary of State for Education* (1989).
46. An Coiste Comhairleach Pleanála / The Advisory Planning Committee, *The Irish Language in a Changing Society: Shaping the Future* (Dublin, Bord na Gaeilge, 1986), pp. xx–xxiii.

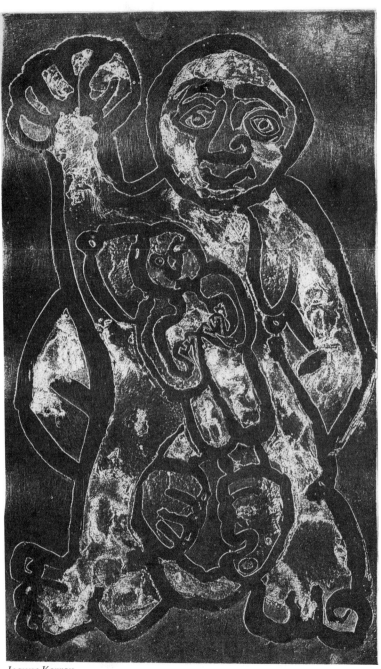

Joanne Karran

9

Field Day's fifth province: avenue or impasse?

Shaun Richards

Seamus Heaney's famous 'Open Letter' of 1983 rebuked the editors of *The Penguin Book of Contemporary British Poetry* for including his poetry in a collection with that title on the grounds that

> My passport's green.
> No glass of ours was ever raised
> To toast *The Queen*.
> . . . [whose] reign
> Of crown and rose
> Defied, displaced, would not combine
> What I'd espouse.

He rejected the appellation 'British' because 'the name's not right'.[1] The 'Open Letter' was published as one of the first of the pamphlet series initiated by the Field Day Theatre Company – of which Heaney is a director – which from its founding in 1980 has developed an ever-more ambitious programme of cultural intervention in the politics of, particularly, Northern Ireland, whose situation it reads as unambiguously colonial. The siting of the Company's base in 'Derry' rather than 'Londonderry' is but one of the indications as to its reading of the Irish situation. The premiers of its plays are in Derry's Guildhall and this, in the words of company director Stephen Rae, 'is a huge symbol of Empire, of the Union, of some kind of adherence to English principles'. There is an irony, as he observed, 'in us doing plays there which maybe undermine that position and certainly come from a different point of view'.[2] Its most recent series (1988) featured work by Fredric Jameson, Terry Eagleton and Edward

Said, whose pamphlet, *Yeats and Decolonization* argued that for those in the Third World Yeats appeared as one who belonged to 'the colonial world ruled by European imperialism'.[3] The probable reasons for the inclusion of Said – articulate supporter of the Palestinian cause – are clarified by the general title of the series in which his work appeared: 'Nationalism, Colonialism and Literature'. This indication of the company's perception of its cultural–political context informs, and problematises, the whole Field Day undertaking.

Although there is no founding manifesto, the introduction to the collection of the company's first six pamphlets, published in 1985 under the title *Ireland's Field Day*, includes a Preface which stated that '[all the directors] believed that Field Day could and should contribute to the solution of the present crisis by producing analyses of the established opinions, myths and stereotypes which had become both a symptom and a cause of the current situation'.[4] The actuality of the 'analysis' of stereotypes is a crucial dimension in this account of Field Day, but one which must be set within the overall definitions of the company which they themselves have provided over the first decade of their operation.

At the heart of the Field Day programme lies the concept of the fifth province. Adopted from the cultural journal *The Crane Bag*, the fifth province was described by Mark Patrick Hederman, one of the journal's co-editors, as 'the secret centre . . . the place where all oppositions were resolved', a definition in accord with his description of *The Crane Bag* itself which could equally be that of the fifth province: 'a no-man's land, a neutral ground, where all things can detach themselves from all partisan and prejudiced connection'.[5] As further defined by Field Day director Tom Paulin, the fifth province 'offers an invisible challenge to the nationalistic image of the four green fields'.[6] But while the nationalist four green fields immortalised in Yeats's *Cathleen Ni Houlihan* are not the ideal (as is clear from the conclusion to Paulin's 1983 poem 'And Where do You Stand on the National Question?'), neither is any idea of remaining 'loose, baggy and British'.[7] The essence of the image, then, is the idea of unity; the fifth province defined in 1984 by Seamus Deane, one of Field Day's directors, and Richard Kearney, one of its contributors, as 'an equivalent centre from which the four broken and fragmented pieces of contemporary Ireland might be seen in fact as coherent'.[8]

The extent to which the fifth province is still at the informing heart of the Field Day enterprise was vividly manifested at the close of the December 1988 BBC 2 *Arena* programme on the company, 'History Boys on the Rampage'. Brian Friel is pictured walking along a beach, his face to the open sea; his voice-over states that Field Day had commissioned plays, pamphlets and translations 'that looked at Ireland from the new perspective, this fifth province, this transcendent location' and from that vantage point they perceived 'vistas that were thrilling, more than thrilling, possible'.[9] The nature of this inherent possibility was made clear during a 1982 interview in which, in answer to the question 'Doesn't the whole Field Day project then depend on political nationalism and on the achievement of a united Ireland?', Friel replied, 'I don't think it should be read in those terms. I think it should lead to a cultural state, not a political state. And I think that out of that cultural state, a possibility of a political state follows'.[10] It is the nature of that political state, effectively predetermined by the cultural state which precedes it, which poses substantial problems of both definition and analysis.

In 1983 Tom Paulin wrote in his poem 'S/He',

It stuck close to me, though,
how all through the last half
    a helicopter held itself
    above the Guildhall –
Vershinin's lines were slewed
by the blind chopping blades,
    though Olga looked chuffed
when she sighed, 'Won't it be odd
with no soldiers on the streets'.[11]

The reference is to the 1981 Field Day production of Friel's version of Chekhov's *Three Sisters*, a choice of play which is perhaps best explained in terms of the reading suggested by Raymond Williams in *Drama From Ibsen to Brecht*. The *Three Sisters*, Williams argued, was perceived as a work containing a new structure of feeling: 'the longing to make sense of life, to have a sense of a future, in a stagnant and boring military-provincial society'.[12] While the sense of Chekhov's play is that the sisters feel deserted and desolate as a result of the garrison's departure, the preferred reading – in Paulin's poem – is that Olga should look 'chuffed' by the troops' withdrawal. It is not that Field Day is a 'nationalist' movement in the sense of being hard-line republican, but there is a real political–cultural consequence of reading Ulster's situation as colonial, in that while there is the desire for a non-sectarian republic ('a form that's classic and secular' in Paulin's terms), there is also the necessity of dealing with those whose sense of political/cultural – and religious – being is predicated upon the maintenance of the fact of Union.

A problematic bias within Field Day was perceived by the poet Eavan Boland at the time of its first pamphlet series in 1983. She commented that 'Judging by the . . . pamphlets here in front of me, this is green nationalism and divided culture'.[13] The difficulty was certainly recognised and acknowledged by Field Day, for, as Seamus Deane observed in 1984, 'It's no good just performing our plays and selling pamphlets to people we know. There's no point in continuing unless we can get through to Unionists'.[14] Field Day addressed this issue most directly in its third pamphlet series (1985), where both Terence Brown and Marianne Elliott attempted to deconstruct the view that Prot-estants were 'inevitably' insular and defensive by recuperating their radical history. In Elliott's words, 'The libertarian thinking behind much of Irish Protestant thinking can, and has, pro-duced dramatic inter-communal alliances and radical solutions in the past and a better understanding of those attitudes might help the quite appreciable merits of that libertarian tradition to rise again in an atmosphere which accepts that the Protestants also need to be conciliated.'[15]

It is the theatrical activity, however, the most public manifest-ation of serious intent, which reveals the greatest difficulties and tensions. For in the same year as the publication of the pamph-lets by Elliott and Brown (1985), Frank McGuiness's play, *Observe the Sons of Ulster Marching Towards the Somme*, was premiered at Dublin's Peacock Theatre after having been offered to Field Day and rejected. In procedural terms this might not be surprising as Field Day normally commissions its plays, the sub-ject and treatment being left very much to the playwright. McGuiness's play – not commissioned, but offered and rejected – becomes problematic, however, because of its content: the play is concerned with the experiences of the Ulster Division at the Battle of the Somme on 1 July 1916, the anniversary of the Battle of the Boyne. The work is a sensitive insight into the cen-trality of sacrifice for the Union upon which claims to selfhood and sovereignty are based. Field Day's non-acceptance of the play recalls the non-production of an earlier work which was commissioned, David Rudkin's *The Saxon Shore*, which was to have appeared in 1983.

More explicitly and empathically than McGuiness, Rudkin also addresses the Protestant predicament. He sets his play at that moment in the fourth century AD when Rome was withdrawing from Britain and the settlers – descendants of those who had come in the wake of conquest – were exposed to the onslaughts of the dispossessed natives. That the play is seen from the stand-point of the settlers is clear from its conclusion. A settler speaks: 'I must wake now. I must wake. Stand. Dig my garden.' The speech is clearly redolent of territorial possession. The final stage-directions read, 'He is standing now, the beginnings of a man'. Rudkin's point of engagement and sympathy is with the settlers' predicament, for as he observed in the Preface to the published text, 'the likelihood almost certainly is that the very first "Saxons" to come here were brought by Rome and planted here: uprooted from their own lands, brought in misery and bondage to a neighbouring island to serve the Empire's cause; then, when Empire's need of them was done, abandoned against the aftermath'.[16]

The company position was that the play was not produced because of a lack of resources, and in that Rudkin's play has fourteen parts there might be a point here. However, at the Almeida Theatre production in 1986 there was considerable doubling, and even trebling, of parts, and only seven actors were involved – a number well within a Field Day norm. According to Rudkin the reason for the rejection was 'literary provisionalism', namely the company's worry about the effect the play would have on republican sensibilities. Rudkin's play was replaced by a production of Athol Fugard's *Boesman and Lena* and, while the idea of an intended parallel between South Africa and Ulster was rejected as 'parochial', the probability of such a reading being made was strong. Indeed it was highly likely. Michael Farrell, a future Field Day pamphleteer, made the analogy in his *Northern Ireland: The Orange State* (1976), and it was reiterated in Declan Kiberd's 1984 Field Day pamphlet *Anglo-Irish Attitudes*.

Debates as to the exclusive nature of the Field Day enterprise and the fifth province have run strongly from the time of the company's first production, Brian Friel's *Translations* (1980). This was criticised – frequently quite savagely – for, among other things, historical inaccuracy, for perpetuating a comforting nationalist idea that the loss of the language and culture was all the fault of the English, and for the naive romanticism of presenting Gaelic culture as a lost Eden. These kinds of arguments have run strongly through the 1980s, most particularly in the critique of Field Day offered by Edna Longley who, in a series of articles and reviews, claimed that the company were 'martyrs to abstraction'. Their opening pamphlet series was 'largely a matter of old whines in new bottles . . . more part of the problem than part of the solution'.[17] She developed the point in a 1985 debate with *The Crane Bag's* Mark Patrick Hederman; it was not the 'admirable notion' of a fifth province which she attacked, 'but the Field Day version and its acceptance as the genuine article'.[18] In her essay, 'Poetry and Politics in Northern Ireland', Longley made the grounds of her objection explicit: Field Day was '[writing] Northern Protestants out of history unless [they were] prepared to go back and start again in 1798'.[19] The significance of the date is the extent to which it has featured for Field Day, particularly in the work of Paulin, as the exemplary moment in which sectarian divisions were subsumed in the desire for a republic freed from British rule. But far from leading Ireland into the future, argued Longley, Field Day '[yearned] for Edenic oneness as opposed to pluralistic "fusion"'.[20]

Longley's position was re-articulated by John Wilson Foster who, in a significant intervention in the debate, asserted that as far as Field Day was concerned, 'Unity is all right, unionism is all wrong'.[21] The work produced by the Field Day enterprise, he claimed, was 'politics by other means'. As 'variations on the nationalist theme [they were] chromatic and resourceful',[22] but what had to be striven for, Foster concluded, was the development of a school of criticism which broke away from unitary thinking. Indeed the essay opened with the assertion that 'The failure of Irish society is the failure of criticism', by which he meant that the divided island had 'supported little criticism that wasn't partisan'.[23] The result, in the case of Field Day, was a sequence of works which, in their nationalist hostility to unionism, '[turned] out to be the political equivalent of male chauvinism'.[24] What had to be attempted was a new and non-partisan enterprise, for 'Success will require getting behind all stereotypes, not just displaying disfavoured stereotypes, as unearned unitary thinking seduces us into doing'.[25]

Foster's essay was delivered at the 1985 conference of the International Association for the Study of Anglo-Irish Literature at Queen's University, Belfast, which was attended by three of

Field Day's directors, and was published in *The Honest Ulsterman* of the same year. Its emphasis on pluralism anticipates the argument put forward by the historian Roy Foster in his address to the 1989 conference on cultural traditions in Ulster, where he attacked as ill-advised the view taken in F. S. L. Lyons's *Culture and Anarchy in Ireland* (1979). Lyons had taken the phrase of the turn-of-the-century polemicist D. P. Moran – 'The Battle of Two Civilizations' – and read recent Irish history in its light, concluding that in Ireland there existed 'an anarchy in the mind and in the heart, an anarchy which forbade not just unity of territories, but also "unity of being", an anarchy that sprang from the collision within a small and intimate island of seemingly irreconcilable cultures . . . caught inextricably in the web of their tragic history'.[26] This, as Foster comments, is 'bleak pessimism'[27] for a 'unilaterally declared nation-statehood [is a] determinist and ideologically redundant notion' in a Europe in which frontiers were falling. In this context 'cultural diversity need not imply political confrontation'.[28]

This idea of a cultural diversity which transcends the old political boundaries has become a feature of much recent debate. It is particularly current in Ireland and is expressed with most conviction by Richard Kearney, ex-editor of *The Crane Bag* and author of one of the first Field Day pamphlets. In his most recent writings Kearney has argued 'not [for] the liquidation of nation but their supercession . . . into a post-nationalist network of communities where national identities may live on where they belong – in languages, sports, arts, customs, memories and myths'.[29] The terms 'post-nationalist', 'trans-nationalist' and 'granular society' run throughout Kearney's work. All suggest a concept he terms 'radical pluralism', which, he believes, can become a reality in which we 'move beyond the established and ultimately failed model of the Nation State towards a society without frontiers'. It is within such a context – one enabled by the EC – that Kearney believes 'Nation States . . . would be superseded [and] an alternative model [would emerge] transcending both the nationalist claim to exclusive unity with the Republic and the unionist claim to exclusive union with Britain'.[30]

The same ideas inform an article in a recent issue of *The Irish Review* by John Wilson Foster in which he also looks to what he terms, somewhat awkwardly, 'a federated archipelago of the future [as] a semi-autonomous region of the EC'.[31] Foster's argument is informed, not only by current ideas of European federalism, but by the work of the Ulster poet John Hewitt, who, from the 1940s, argued for a regional culture in which both Planter and Gael could be recognised. As Hewitt expressed it in 1972, there is a moment 'when a colony set among an older population ceases simply to be a colony and becomes something else . . . a valid region with the inalienable right to choose its place within a smaller or larger federation'.[32] This desired transcendence of old categories and old divisions, particularly those which are presented as absolute in their determining force, runs parallel to the practice of contemporary historians whose research, Roy Foster argues, has questioned the rigid 'landlord-versus-tenant, orange-versus-green patterns of the old text-books'. This reductive reading he observes, is 'now adhered to only by wishful-thinking English and American observers'.[33] In the advance publicity for *The Field Day Anthology of Irish Literature 550 AD-1980* (for publication in Autumn 1990) Seamus Deane, the anthology's editor, states that the company sees the collection as an important act of definition that will show how the various groups, sects and races which have intermingled in Ireland have produced a literature that is unique to them and an achievement which makes manifest what they have in common'.[34] This might appear to endorse Longley's criticism that the company are more concerned with unity than plurality, but Tom Paulin's comments, in interview, clearly suggest an understanding of the need to recognise difference. He noted that the intention was 'not to really privilege one tradition over the other'; not to present an ideology, but ideologies, and say to the reader 'make what you want of them'.[35] The anthology becomes, in this sense, a representation of plurality in the very richness of its literary representations.

Paulin was speaking about the forthcoming anthology at London's Royal Festival Hall in the same month that Field Day came to the Hampstead Theatre with their production of Terry Eagleton's *Saint Oscar*. While the staged play revealed significant differences from the published text in terms of the areas addressed below – and this might reveal a sensitivity within the company which exceeded that of their collaborators – an examin-ation of the text of the play, published under the Field Day imprint in 1989, highlights the continuing problem of the exclusivism of the fifth province.

Eagleton's introduction to the published edition speaks of 'colonial oppression', the 'colonial oppressor', the 'colonial subject' and 'the experience of colonialism',[36] and claims contemporary relevance for the play. In Eagleton's words, 'Oscar Wilde's treatment at the hands of a brutal, arrogant British establishment is being acted out once more in Ireland today, with brutality of a different kind'.[37] In the aftermath of the quashing of the Guildford Four convictions, the fact of brutality in Ireland and the judicial persecution of the Irish can no longer be disputed, but what is striking is the way in which Eagleton reads the contemporary situation – 'small nations will not rest until they are free'[38] – and the dramatic representation of those who, implicitly, are the enslavers. At the close of the play Edward Carson, Wilde's prosecutor and future leader of Ulster Protestantism, speaks: 'this is our territory: British soil. Our fathers planted and nurtured it and handed it down to us as a sacred trust'. As Carson concludes, the stage directions read, 'Lights up on Chorus, standing round CARSON in paramilitary uniform, head masks with eye-holes. Drums, union jacks. Drum roll'.[39]

Eagleton's concept of an unfree 'nation' enchained by Protestant militarism clearly struck a responsive chord in the mind of his director, Trevor Griffiths, who, in his contribution to *The Guardian* Diary in September 1989, provided what could easily be taken as a parody of British left-wing perceptions of Protestant Ulster. In this world, according to Griffiths, 'moneys are raised, covenants sworn, plots hatched, surrenders negatived'; the idea that the swearing of the covenant has been a feature of Protestant life since 1912 parallels Eagleton's own compression of history in which Carson merges with contemporary paramilitaries – all frozen in the 'colonial' moment. While Protestants are viewed by Griffiths as inhabiting streets through which one wouldn't care to walk alone after dark, the Catholics have resistance 'bred . . . in the bone and on the tongue'. Their city (Derry) is one of 'verve and wit and resilience'; Ireland itself is a place where 'a song well-aimed can still be as deadly as a bullet'.[40] Here 'the established opinions, myths and stereotypes' would appear to be perpetuated rather than dispelled, and Griffiths and (to a lesser extent) Eagleton only provide evidence for those like the late Unionist MP Harold McCusker, who, even before such pronouncements, read Field Day as imbued with 'nationalist' sentiment. He did, as he observed, find 'some question marks' hanging over the work of the company as it seemed to him concerned 'sometimes subtly, sometimes not so subtly, to knock things unionist'; a reading which itself becomes an argument for a reinforcement of sectarian absolutes.[41]

The Field Day ideal of the fifth province justifies the description of the company advanced by the playwright Thomas Kilroy when he spoke of it as 'a platform for the life of the mind, of whatever persuasion, at a time when mindlessness threatens to engulf us all'.[42] In the pamphlets, particularly those of Terence Brown and Marianne Elliott, it has engaged in an analysis of stereotypes, and, if it follows the concept of 'radical pluralism' articulated by one member of its 'invisible college', Richard Kearney, one can see the prospect of Field Day contributing to, as the company phrased it, 'the solution of the present crisis'. In this reading, the exclusivist, unitary nature of some fifth-province thinking would seem to be a stage of development, a necessary prelude to a recognition of the possibilities inherent in the 1990s, a decade informed by considerations which were dormant, rather than non-existent, in the decade of the company's foundation. What is regrettable, however, and what is worrying is that aspects of its latest theatrical work appear to have succumbed to the limitations of its sympathisers, who, to adapt Roy Foster's comment, are less analysts than 'wishful-thinking English observers' bound up in a '[too] neatly demarcated' pattern of 'orange-versus-green' beloved by 'the old textbooks'.

References

1. Seamus Heaney, 'An Open Letter', Field Day Theatre Company, *Ireland's Field Day* (London, 1985), pp. 25–6.
2. 'History Boys on the Rampage', BBC 2 *Arena* programme on Field Day Theatre Company, broadcast December 1988.
3. Edward Said, *Yeats and Decolonization* (Derry, 1988), p. 5.
4. Preface, *Ireland's Field Day*, p. vii.
5. Mark Patrick Hederman, 'Poetry and the Fifth Province', *The Crane Bag*, Vol. 9, No. 1, 1985, p. 110.
6. Tom Paulin, Introduction, *Ireland and the English Crisis* (Newcastle-upon-Tyne, 1984), p. 17.
7. Tom Paulin, 'And Where Do You Stand on the National Question?', *Liberty Tree* (London, 1983), p. 68.
8. Seamus Deane and Richard Kearney, 'Why Ireland Needs a Fifth Province', *The Sunday Independent*, 22 January 1984.
9. History Boys on the Rampage, note 2.

10. 'The Man From God Knows Where', an interview with Brian Friel by Fintan O'Toole, *In Dublin*, No. 165, 1982, p. 23.

11. Tom Paulin, 'S/He', *Liberty Tree*, p. 73.

12. Raymond Williams, *Drama From Ibsen to Brecht* (London, 1987), p. 107. The relevance of Williams's comment to Field Day is made clear by Eamonn Hughes in '"To Define Your Dissent": The Plays and Polemics of the Field Day Theatre Company', *Theatre Research International*, Vol. 15, No. 1, Spring 1990, p. 72.

13. Eavan Boland, 'Poets and Pamphlets', *The Irish Times*, 1 October 1983.

14. Deane and Kearney, note 8.

15. Marianne Elliott, *Watchmen in Sion: The Protestant Idea of Liberty* (Derry, 1985), p. 27.

16. David Rudkin, *The Saxon Shore* (London, 1986), p. vii.

17. Edna Longley, 'More Martyrs to Abstraction', *Fortnight*, July/August 1984, p. 20.

18. Edna Longley, 'A Reply', *The Crane Bag*, Vol. 9, No. 1, 1985, p. 120.

19. Edna Longley, 'Poetry and Politics in Northern Ireland', *Poetry in The Wars* (Newcastle-upon-Tyne, 1986), p. 192.

20. Longley, note 19, p. 196.

21. John Wilson Foster, 'The Critical Condition of Ulster', *The Honest Ulsterman*, 79, Autumn 1985, p. 43.

22. Foster, note 21, p. 45.

23. Foster, note 21, pp. 38–9.

24. Foster, note 21, p. 44.

25. Foster, note 21, p. 46.

26. F. S. L. Lyons, *Culture and Anarchy in Ireland 1890–1939* (Oxford, 1982), p. 177.

27. Roy Foster, 'Inaugural Lecture', in Martin Crozier, ed., *Cultural Traditions in Northern Ireland* (Belfast, 1989), p. 6.

28. Foster, note 27, p. 22.

29. Richard Kearney, 'Introduction: Thinking Otherwise', in Richard Kearney, ed., *Across the Frontiers: Ireland in the 1990s* (Dublin, 1988), p. 17.

30. Kearney, note 29, p. 18.

31. John Wilson Foster, 'Radical Regionalism', *The Irish Review*, 7, Autumn 1989, p. 7.

32. John Hewitt, 'No Rootless Colonist', in Tom Clyde, ed., *Ancestral Voices: The Selected Prose of John Hewitt* (Belfast, 1987), p. 156.

33. Foster, note 27, p. 12.

34. Field Day publicity brochure.

35. 'History Boys on the Rampage', note 2.

36. Terry Eagleton, *Saint Oscar* (Derry, 1989), pp. x–xi.

37. Eagleton, note 36, p. xi.

38. Eagleton, note 36, p. xii.
39. Eagleton, note 36, p. 61–2.
40. Trevor Griffiths, 'Tales of derring-do on the Derry stage', Diary, *The Guardian* (Review), 23–24 September, 1989, p. 5.
41. 'History Boys on the Rampage', note 2.
42. Thomas Kilroy, 'Author's Note', *Double Cross* programme.

10

Intellectuals and political culture: a unionist-nationalist comparison

Liam O'Dowd

The political impasse

To outsiders the inability of unionists and nationalists in Ireland to engage in constructive political dialogue is mystifying. One of the explanations most frequently advanced is the existence of political violence. Yet the rejection of dialogue preceded the 'troubles'. Over forty years were to elapse before the prime ministers of both parts of Ireland met. When their meeting finally occurred it generated internal upheaval within unionism and arguably contributed to the disintegration of the Stormont system. The minimal level of political negotiation between unionism and nationalism appears to lend credence to the views of those who argue that the conflict is over essentially 'non-bargainable' issues such as nationality and religion. A somewhat more positive version of this analysis allows that the issue is one of conflicting identities.[1]

More recently, the British and Irish governments also appear to have adopted an increasingly sceptical view about the prospects for internal political dialogue in Northern Ireland. Whatever the intentions of its drafters, the Anglo-Irish Agreement is a remarkable institutionalisation of such scepticism. It seems to acknowledge the improbability of any durable settlement emerging from political negotiations between the unionist and nationalist parties. As such it marks a major piece of political revisionism – an abandonment by the British government of any 'purely internal and British solution' to the Northern conflict and a similar

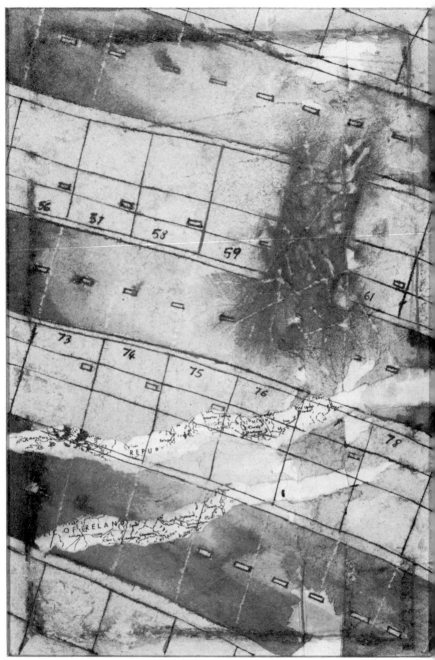

Paul Pickersgill

abandonment by the Irish government of a solution 'internal to Ireland' without British involvement.

While the Agreement has scarcely mobilised widespread support in Northern Ireland, neither has it provoked sustained opposition on the streets. It has engendered grudging compliance rather than mass legitimation. This outcome suggests perhaps that a majority in Northern Ireland share one of the premises of the Agreement – that prospects for substantive political dialogue between unionists and nationalists are poor. Of course, this consensus does not imply agreement on the reasons for the political impasse: some point to the hindrance of existing political frameworks, while others argue that military victory must precede political dialogue.[2]

This article seeks to probe one reason for the historical limits on political dialogue. This is the differential role and ideology of intellectuals within unionism and nationalism. Unionism, I will suggest, is a movement in which political intellectuals have been traditionally marginalised and constrained by popular political culture. Nationalism, on the other hand, has allowed a much more autonomous role to intellectuals. While one effect is to make Irish nationalism more comprehensible and communicable to the outside world, another seems to be a gulf between the role and ideology of unionist and nationalist intellectuals. This article explores some of the reasons for the gulf and considers the way in which it contributes to a climate which precludes constructive political negotiation.

The role and ideology of intellectuals

There is an embryonic awareness among nationalists, unionists and outside observers that the different ideologies and political roles of intellectuals may be a significant feature in the political impasse in Ireland. Liberal nationalists are inclined to see the problem in terms of a lack of rational intellectual discourse within unionism. *The Irish Times*, in advising Mrs Thatcher on how to deal with the opposition of unionists to the Anglo-Irish Agreement, observed,

> They do not practise politics as do she and her colleagues.
> They are wont to conduct their politics as if it were a series of
> revival meetings. There is one theme only, there is no

questioning or trading – only preaching, enthusiasm and zeal.

Terence Brown blames unionist political ideology for simplifying and stereotyping the historical experience of Ulster Protestants. He suggests that, in contrast to the history of Irish nationalism, that of Protestants, is 'starkly simple in outline and depressingly lacking in emotional range and complexity'.[3] For Brown even the rich and diverse Presbyterian tradition has been overcome by 'a vision of the Northern Protestant as having always belonged to a homogenous, ideologically monolithic social group which stands for authority, law, order, loyalty, conformity, social cohesion and reason'(p. 11).

Another observer, Desmond Bell, who like Brown has a Northern Protestant background, underlines the pre-eminence of popular culture within unionism. He suggests that the Lambeg drum, the summer marches and the ostentatious identification with the flag and with flaunting dominance are all more important than political ideology.[4]

In a critique of Ulster unionism which manages to be at once hostile, sympathetic and patronising, Tom Nairn argues that 'bible fundamentalism and Union Jackery made impossible the development of a normal national intelligentsia'. The 'absence of an intellectual class' explains, in his view, 'the bowler-hatted inarticulacy of the [unionist] community in a public or historical sense'.[5] For Nairn, the pathological assymetry of the Irish Question is that Protestants have been unable to develop a fully-fledged modern Ulster nationalism. Miller in a more compelling historical analysis suggests that evangelicalism and Presbyterian contractarianism have acted as substitutes for nationalism. The latter 'was pressed into service to sacralize the state conceived in 1912 and born in 1921. The myth system failed, not because its ordinary adherents lost faith in it, but because its elite drifted away'.[6] After 1921, as the literary critic (and Ulster Protestant) John Wilson Foster puts it:

> Ulster did not need thinkers or apologists. It was on automatic pilot, set by grey and visionless men. Unionism as an intellectually defensible or culturally defensible belief withered away.[7]

Another participant in the 'one versus two nations' debate has denounced the Protestant middle classes and the Stormont government in particular for failing to have its hired intellectuals like other governments, thus leaving unionism 'undefended in the war of cultural propaganda'.[8]

Although there is little common ground between these observers in terms of the scope or nature of their analyses; there is a measure of consensus on the absence of an Ulster nationalism and the lack of political intellectuals to articulate it. The superficial consensus is, however, exploded by the rather contradictory solutions proposed. Nairn, on the basis of precious little evidence, discerns the beginnings of an Ulster nationalism; 'integrationists' prescribe the importation of a British nationalism via the 'national parties' to overcome parochial sectarian squabbles, while cultural analysts call variously for redefinitions of Ulster, Irish and/or British identity. Many of the latter, loosely following Miller's 'no-nation', thesis suggest that nationalism is *passé* in any case.

Most of these analyses imply a contrast between Irish nationalism and Ulster unionism even though they are seen as defining each other. The articulacy of the former is contrasted with the inarticulacy of the latter; and the relative success of nationalist propaganda is contrasted with the failure of unionism to mobilise sympathetic responses in Britain or abroad.

Such generalisations, however plausible, are seldom supported by rigorous analysis. While unionism may lack prominent political intellectuals, it does not lack an intelligentsia.[9] The term 'intelligentsia' is sometimes used in a much narrower sense to indicate critical or dissenting intellectuals. Here it is used in its wider sociological meaning, while the term 'intellectual' is defined more narrowly but in such a way as to include critics and supporters of established authority. This distinction is useful in understanding the contrasting role and ideology of intellectuals in nationalism and unionism. All modern societies contain a growing intelligentsia performing managerial, administrative, academic and technical roles. These include clergy, academics, engineers, scientists, doctors, managers, trade unionists and political activists. The intelligentsia is formed by the increasing division of labour and by differentiation of mental from manual labour. Membership is increasingly tied to educational credentials.

Intellectuals, on the other hand, are typically members of the intelligentsia who concern themselves with social questions beyond the remit of their own specialised area of knowledge. In so doing they may draw on a general moral or humanistic position or build outwards from their own specialisms. Political intellectuals attempt to speak to global, national, class or communal concerns, or to a combination of these issues.[10] There is no non-problematical definition of intellectual in this sense: it is a politically contested term, not only by other intellectuals, but also by other elements of the social structure. Furthermore, the label itself is often avoided by intellectuals themselves because of its esoteric and elitist connotations.

In mediating between the rulers and the ruled, intellectuals help to shape political culture by generating a political discourse. This is simultaneously a form of self-definition and legitimation as well as an attempt to assert the legitimacy or otherwise of those who wield power. Intellectuals also make implicit or explicit claims in the name of their proficiency in art, literature, science or technical matters, to distinguish themselves from non-intellectuals. While they may claim to be professionals in their own field, they seek to express interests and beliefs, and to address audiences, beyond those of their own occupational groupings. With the growth of the professional intelligentsia in all modern societies, intellectuals are increasingly influenced by the tension between professional/technical expertise on the one hand, and the more traditional intellectual activity of proclaiming broad political and moral positions on the other. Furthermore, the composition of the professional intelligentsia influences the ideology and role of political intellectuals, and the intelligentsia, in turn, are products of wider social structures.

Nationalism versus unionism; a structural comparison

Therefore, in assessing the role of unionist and nationalist intellectuals, it is necessary to locate them within a wider class and institutional framework. The structural differences between nationalist and unionist Ireland have been well rehearsed. The uneven development of industrial capitalism in Ireland generated a social structure in the North built around a substantial industrial working class and a diverse bourgeoisie composed of landed gentry, entrepreneurs and professionals. In the South, the urban working class was smaller, less industrial and more dispersed. There was a much larger and differentiated farming class and a middle class dominated by a small businessmen and professionals.

From very different starting points at partition, however, the

Table 1   Professions as a percentage of the gainfully occupied

	Irish Republic	Northern Ireland
1926	4.2 (55,441)	3.2 (18,141)
1951	5.9 (74,654)	5.0 (30,100)
1971	9.2 (103,316)	11.0 (60,011)
1981	12.2 (154,518)	14.3 (89,848)

Source: Census of Northern Ireland and Irish Republic

industrial profile of both parts of Ireland has tended to converge: agriculture has greatly contracted, manufacturing now accounts for the same proportion of employees in each area, and there has been a dramatic expansion in (the state-dominated) service sector.[11] While statistical convergence is not to be identified with a convergence of class relations, it is clear that structural conditions in both North and South, as in other industrial societies, have been favourable to the growth of a professional stratum. Taking the census definitions of 'professional and technical occupations' as a rather crude and imperfect index of an intelligentsia, Table 1 details its growth since 1926.

Generally, there has been a faster growth of professional occupations in the North from a position where it lagged behind the South in 1926. This is in part due to the faster growth of the state and services sector in the North in line with that in Britain generally.

Table 2   Changing composition of professional category

Per cent of total 1981	1926		1951		1971		1981	
Professions	IR	NI	IR	NI	IR	NI	IR	NI
Clergy	26	10	39	8	19	4	10	2
Teachers	31	46	21	31	24	31	27	28
Judges/doctors/ barristers	6	8	7	7	6	4	6	5
Engineers/scientists	3	3	4	6	6	11	6	6

Source: Census of Northern Ireland and Irish Republic

There are, however, marked differences between North and South in the occupational composition of the professional intelligentsia over time (Table 2). The most striking point of contrast here is the significance of the clergy in the South and their rapid relative decline in recent decades. In proportionate terms, the clergy are between 2.5 and 5 times more significant in the Southern intelligentsia than in its Northern counterpart – a gap which would be wider if northern Protestants were compared separately with the South. The table also indicates the increasing differentiation of both intelligentsias as the proportion of the major blocs (clergy and teachers) declines.[12]

The impact of the intelligentsia on Irish politics

Professionals have been heavily over-represented among politicians from both unionist and nationalist traditions. Chubb has commented that 'at the top of [Southern] Irish politics the domination of professional men is overwhelming'. Over 60 per cent of all cabinet ministers between 1922 and 1979 were professionals, although their representation among the gainfully occupied ranged from only 4 to 14 per cent.[13] Professionals accounted for a somewhat smaller percentage (41 per cent) in unionist cabinets between 1921 and 1969.[14]

The unionist-nationalist difference is magnified when the leadership of both governments are considered. Unionist prime ministers were drawn exclusively from the large landowner/industrialist group. This group also controlled 41 per cent of all cabinet posts and the key ministry of finance. The occupational contrast between Craig, Andrews, Brooke, O'Neill, Chichester-Clark and Faulkner on the one hand, and Cosgrave, De Valera, Costello, Lemass, Lynch, Haughey, and Fitzgerald on the other is quite striking. No professional or intellectual has ever led the Unionist Party since partition.[15]

It might be argued that as Stormont was a local administration the appropriate comparison might be with local government in the South where the impact of farmers and businessmen was greater.[16] Certainly there are similarities in the clientelism and pragmatism operating at this level – yet even here, in contrast to the unionists, nationalists both North and South were skewed towards the lower end of the small business/farming group. The structure of the Unionist Party was more like that of their close allies the British Conservative Party than that of any of the Irish

nationalist parties. It is significant, of course, that big businessmen and landowners have largely withdrawn from active
electoral politics since the abolition of Stormont.

There is considerable evidence that the indirect influence of the
professions on unionist and nationalist politics was different
also. The impact of the smaller number of clergy on unionist
politics was mediated through the Orange order – lay Protestants
were made more responsible for defending politico-religious
principles than lay Catholics. Not only were Protestant clergy less
numerous, they were less keen than their Catholic counterparts
to inform political life with a coherent social philosophy. As
political lobbyists, they concentrated on fairly specific issues
relating to education, temperance, sabbatarianism and welfare
services.[17] Unlike the Catholic clergy, some Protestant ministers
were elected to parliament, but they were seldom part of the
unionist leadership until the 1970s. In many ways the pervasive
ideological influence of the Catholic church on nationalist politics
precluded the need for involvement in electoral politics. The
more far-reaching control by the Catholic clergy of the teaching
profession, and of the form and content of the curriculum
ensured intimate church-state relations. The expanding number
of clerical professionals in the thirty years after partition coincided with the church's project of building a Catholic social order
in the South.[18] The impact of this on the 1937 Constitution, the
censorship campaign, and debates over health, social services
and vocational organisation has been thoroughly documented.[19]

Nor was there any parallel in unionist politics to the prominence of teachers' organisations in politics as in the case of the
rise of Clann na Poblachta in the late 1940s. In any case, in the
North, the major clerical and teaching professions were split on
sectarian grounds, thus marginalising the political impact of both
Catholics and the professions taken as a whole. Again, the role of
Stormont in mainly administering legislation initiated in Britain
further reduced scope for professional contributions, or for broad
ideological debate, on the merits of government policy.

The different professional/intellectual orientations to politics
can also be traced to systemic differences in the Protestant and
Catholic educational systems. The Catholic educational system
has been biased historically towards the arts and humanities
compared to the more scientific and technical orientation of its
Protestant counterpart. Historically, Protestants and unionists
dominated Irish science and technology.[20] This cultural bias

continues to find an echo within the Northern Ireland intelligentsia today. Evidence on subjects studied in secondary schools in the North, and on university subjects studied in British and Irish universities since 1960, shows persisting Catholic–Protestant differences even if there are now some signs of convergence.[21]

Until recently, at least, scientists and technical experts have had little direct input into nationalist or unionist politics. In any case, they are likely to be less overtly political. Their claims to expertise relate to more specific knowledge than humanistic intellectuals, and their frame of reference is more likely to transcend small political units like Northern Ireland and the Republic. Protestant intellectual bias toward science and technical subjects accentuates the 'apolitical' role of the unionist intelligentsia. The activities of humanistic intellectuals, on the other hand, relate more directly to states as political units and to the formulation of political ideologies. In either case, the role and ideology of intellectuals cannot be understood apart from the political, institutional and class structures of which they are a part.

Intellectuals and political ideology

Unlike Irish nationalists, unionists never actively sought a separate sovereign state in order to accomplish specific economic, political or cultural goals. From the outset, the state was not perceived as a positive initiating agent, but rather as a bulwark against Catholicism and nationalism. Its intellectuals, as part of either a British or Ulster framework, had no language to revive and no sustained critique of foreign oppression. In 'inventing its tradition' it neither romanticised its peasantry nor linked its local folklore to a national cultural ideal. As Desmond Bell has observed, 'we'll find no Hyde or Pearse on the streets of Portadown'.[22]

In opposition to Nairn, however, it may be suggested that unionists did not lack intellectuals so much as a particular type of humanist intellectual prominent in Irish and other nationalist movements. Lack of a 'normal' national identity constructed by intellectuals should not be confused with the lack of an articulated social identity of an ethnic-religious nature. Furthermore, it must be recognised that this identity was forged in historical interaction with, and in opposition to, the nationalist and

Catholic movement in Ireland. As an 'imagined community' in Benedict Anderson's sense[23], its self-image as a colony was important, as was its openness to the frequently racist ideology of British imperialism in the nineteenth century. The reasons for its failure to develop a coherent national ideology must be located not only in the social structure of the North, but also in its historic monopoly of local power, held with the support of, and on behalf of, the British state in Ireland.

The historical prominence of intellectuals in the revolutionary elite of Irish nationalism has been thoroughly documented.[24] In this, Ireland fitted an international pattern. All the major analyses of modern nationalist movements have detailed the crucial role of intellectuals, especially those of a literary and humanistic orientation.[25] This role has been more autonomous in regions with a similar class structure to nationalist Ireland, with large farming populations, a dispersed urban working class with limited industrial experience, and a substantial commercial and small business class.[26] In settings such as these with typically high levels of literacy, nationalist intellectuals often acted as a political vanguard. In Ireland they sought to construct an inclusive political ideology which would appeal to various class fragments and to the local and religious movements which coexisted in Ireland. National separatism had received its first modern definition and leadership from northern Presbyterians. But nationalism and republicanism had to contend with two popular mass movements which were antithetical to each other, nineteenth-century Catholicism and Orangeism.

The political and class forces which led to the coalescing of Protestantism and unionism on the one hand and Catholicism and nationalism on the other have been well chronicled by Irish historians. Nevertheless, Protestant intellectuals had played a leading role in developing nineteenth- and early twentieth-century cultural identity and nationalism.[27] It was only for a brief period that a relatively unified Irish 'imagined community' was created among Irish intellectuals. This originated in the cultural revivals, archaeological and antiquarian researchers of the nineteenth century and assumed its most definitive shape between 1890 and 1930. By then it incorporated a variety of overlapping movements, the Anglo-Irish literary renaissance, the Gaelic League, the Cooperative Movement, the suffragist movement, Sinn Fein and the Irish socialist movement. Its intellectuals were drawn from all parts of the social structure (although not proportionately) – church of Ireland gentry and professions, the Presbyterian middle class, the rural middle classes and the urban working class.[28] For a time it comprised both nationalist and unionist but it was not coherent or active as a political entity.

Ultimately, key elements in this intellectual stratum were to support the separatist movement in which teachers, writers and poets were prominent among the leadership. Their political achievement was the mobilisation of mass support with the (at first) ambiguous support of the Catholic clergy. Thereafter, church and state began to give a definite shape to the political role of intellectuals in the Free State in politics, the educational system and the new state administration. Writers appealing to the broader traditions of the pre-partition intelligentsia assumed the role of dissenters. Intellectual disillusionment was focused on the new clerical and political establishment, however, rather than on the northern unionist regime. The latter owed little to politicised intellectuals and never raised expectations of a new social order in the first place.

Southern political parties did not divide on 'right/left' lines, they reflected Civil War divisions and operated a pragmatic and clientelist form of politics. Yet alongside this apparently anti-intellectual and often populist form of politics, there were a series of intense political and intellectual debates. These dealt with topics such as censorship, the Catholic corporatist ideal, the language revival, emigration, economic stagnation, planning and health care. Furthermore, the definition of Irish national identity and its relationship to the the wider world remained an issue. There was no comparable dimension to politics in the North.

Protestant Ulster was now disassociated from its most politically-oriented intellectuals. Some had allied themselves to Irish nationalism, if only temporarily. Others subscribed to a wider, if now crumbling, imperial ideal. Writers and poets identified with wider British literary traditions or with the Anglo-Irish literary tradition. Small groups of liberal and radical intellectuals survived within the confines of the Presbyterian church and the labour movement. Catholic intellectuals remained voluntarily or involuntarily the servants of their own community. In higher education, the influence of Scottish and later English educationalists was strong and they had little intellectual or political interest in local affairs.[29] Similar influences were evident in the local BBC, which until the 1960s contrived to avoid dealing with

any local issues which might be regarded as remotely contentious.[30]

Northern Ireland politics was dominated by the landed gentry
and local industrialists whose legitimacy had a dual basis. They
operated a system of patronage for their working-class support
and subscribed to popular Orangeism as the cultural basis of the
new political unit. That this popular political culture is not easily
seen as rational by intellectuals is no accident. It is not unrelated
to the subordinate and marginal role of political intellectuals
within the unionist movement. The key role of intellectuals as
political educators so prominent in liberal democratic, nationalist
and socialist movements is largely absent here. Furthermore,
unlike the Catholic church, the Protestant churches did not
provide a clerical model of professional privilege and status for
other intellectuals intent on contributing to political debate.

Intellectuals and the Northern crisis

The eruption of the Northern crisis laid bare the scope (and the
limits) of intellectuals' impact on political culture. The importance of intellectuals and professionals in formulating and pub-
licising civil rights demands became obvious, but, eventually, so
too did their limitations. Programmatic demands for reform were
no substitute for the power to realise them. For many of the
structural reasons discussed above, nationalist intellectuals received little support from unionist intellectuals. Instead they
provoked intense *popular* unionist opposition. This opened the
way for a popular nationalist response under the aegis of the IRA.
While professionals and intellectuals typically distanced themselves from the IRA, the latter's activities, however objectionable
they might seem, were still more readily (and perhaps too easily)
understood than those of their loyalist and unionist opponents.
The political language of nationalism and republicanism was a
more accessible intellectual currency than that of Paisley and the
UDA.

The burgeoning international media and social science interest
in Northern Ireland was reflected in an apparently endless
stream of sponsored seminars in Ireland, Britain and the US,
where, it was hoped, the contending parties might resolve their
differences in rational discussion. The major impetus was of
course the apparent anomaly of mass political violence within the
broader American–western European context. From an early

preoccupation with the Catholic and nationalist case, attention began to be diverted to the 'real kernel of the problem'. This was the virulent popular opposition of loyalists to the more readily understandable demands of nationalists for equitable partici-pation in state institutions. A gap between the comprehensibility of both sides began to appear. While students of Irish nationalism could fall back on a host of conventional literary sources, political histories, pamphlets and creative literature, information on loyalism was not so easily accessible. This in turn opened the way for closer examination of the Ulster unionist community. Not surprisingly, the new research favoured more ethnographic methods and sources such as Orange songs, Free Presbyterian sermons, banners, graffiti and popular newspapers. One of the unintended effects of this research has been to illuminate the position of intellectuals vis-a-vis unionist political culture.

The researchers set out to make loyalism comprehensible in terms of 'rational' intellectual discourse. While Richard Rose had already delineated the political attitudes of the 'Protestant ultras' in his survey in the late 1960s, popular loyalism now came in for more sustained empirical scrutiny.[31] The object was to make sense of what Geoff Bell termed 'the most misunderstood and criticised community in western Europe'. Sarah Nelson aptly summarises the problem of comprehensibility:

> They [the loyalists] are loyal to Britain, yet ready to disobey her; they reject clerical tyranny, yet oppose secularism; they proclaim an ideology of freedom and equality, except for Catholics; they revere law and authority, then break the law. And they refuse to do the rational obvious thing.[32]

What these accounts show *inter alia* is the way in which these ideas, apparently in opposition at the abstract level, are recon-ciled at the level of direct and popular political *activity*. They show the centrality of Orange marches, of the mobilising power of Paisley's revivalist style, of confrontations with Catholics, of the flags, arches and graffiti in delineating loyalist territory. To working-class Catholics this is merely supremacism, to loyalists it is an important part of their social and political identity.

The research of Desmond Bell, Nelson, Jenkins, Bruce and others reveals the various interlocking strands of popular loyal-ism as an ideology – its evangelical Protestantism, anti-Catholicism, racist views of Catholics as 'filthy Fenian scum', the feeling of being 'outbred', a proletarian suspicion of the 'fur-coat brigade', yet a deep suspicion of socialism, its sense of being an 'elect' and embattled people with a mission of recalling the British state to its old political and religious values. Overall adherence to communal exclusivism is linked to an understanding of 'the privileges of British citizenship as *exclusive entitlements* bequested to Protestants qua Protestants rather than as *inclusive rights* afforded to every member of a country'.[33] Clearly, the gulf between this popular exclusivism and the inclusive ideology of many liberal-democratic, socialist and nationalist intellectuals is considerable.

It may be argued that all popular *political* ideologies contain contradictory and exclusivistic elements. In the case of unionism, however, intellectuals have failed to forge an enduring link between a popular political culture and any major political ideology such as liberal democracy, socialism or nationalism.[34] Part of the reason for this is the popular and visual, rather than literary or intellectual, nature of loyalist culture. As Bell observes, 'it is the sound of the Lambeg drum, rather than the resonance of political ideology, which bring tears to the eyes of a Loyalist'.[35]

More importantly, perhaps, popular loyalism is not easily translatable into a mere collection of abstract ideas because it has proved too successful as a vehicle of popular *power*. Loyalists have had much better reasons than nationalists for believing in the efficacy of direct action as opposed to that of ideological programmes. Popular loyalism has long been an integral element in the general practice of political power in Northern Ireland – the unionist leadership's manipulation of sectarian geography to ensure unionist control of votes, housing and jobs. Furthermore, it would be misleading to suggest that Direct Rule has made redundant the popular politics of territorial control in the North. They continue to structure inter-communal conflict and events such as the loyalist general strikes. But loyalists have been incorporated and used by the British administration to manage the conflict via the 'Ulsterisation' of the security forces, albeit not on terms fully acceptable to those who advocate more 'shoot-to-kill' policies.

Nevertheless, the material conditions and the parameters within which popular loyalism operates have changed significantly. It is not married to formal adminstrative practices as it was under Stormont – at best it retains the power of popular veto *in extremis*. These changed circumstances have implications for the political role of intellectuals.

A new role for intellectuals?

This article has argued that one of the key differences between unionist and nationalist political culture has been reflected in the political role of intellectuals. The class, institutional and political context of unionism has marginalised political intellectuals, making it difficult to link popular loyalism to broader political ideologies. The role of intellectuals in the political structure of nationalist Ireland has been stronger. This has allowed for a much closer integration of political ideology and popular culture.

Since the 1960s, major changes in the parameters of Irish politics, North and South, have set new political challenges for intellectuals. Again, nationalist intellectuals have been much more prominent than their unionist counterparts in meeting these changes. In some respects, these challenges have been common to both parts of Ireland, insofar as they have included the impact of multi-national corporations, growing state involvement in the economy and everyday life, and membership of the EC.

In the South, Catholic-nationalist ideologies dominant since partition have been revised in response to these changes. These changes have included a subtle, but nevertheless thoroughgoing, downgrading of the 'national question'. Clerical intellectuals, so dominant for thirty years after the Treaty, have moved sideways. They have been joined, and to some extent replaced, by a more diverse and secular intelligentsia located principally within greatly expanded state institutions. They move more freely than before within a broader international context which includes the US, the UK and the EC generally. The New Ireland Forum represented an attempt by the new political and intellectual dispensation to deal with some unfinished business inherited from the old. And, indeed, the Report sought to re-interpret traditional nationalist views in the context of changed conditions.

At the outset, in the North, the marginal stratum of unionist intellectuals were ill-equipped to deal with the changing parameters of local politics. In addition to challenges from the South, these included the Civil Rights movement, the Provisional IRA, the sudden glare of international attention and, perhaps most importantly of all, direct British government involvement. Despite the attempts of various modernising intellectuals and politicians, including the ecumenically-minded clergy, the New Ulster Movement and other advocates of a more inclusive unionism, the new challenges were re-interpreted within the frame of popular loyalism. They were seen mainly as a mixture of republican sedition, unionist 'Lundys' and British duplicity.

The nationalist-republican response was much more multi-dimensional. It included the liberal-democratic and reformist claims of the Civil Rights movement, the SDLP and elements in Southern politics. Traditional republicans succeeded in mobilising significant working-class support while incorporating elements of socialist ideology. Finally, the Catholic church was able to rely on its considerable experience of linking absolutist religious principles with political ambiguity.[36]

The nationalist response was infinitely more attuned to contributions from intellectuals, to communicating with international opinion, and to political negotiation and compromise. It must be added that this emphasis has an historical and contemporary root in the incapacity of nationalists to enforce their preferred solution by coercion.

For Ulster unionists, the possibilities of coercion had not been so limited. Coercion, or the threat of coercion, rather than compromise or negotiation had been the basis of the Stormont system for fifty years. Unlike nationalists, unionists had found it unnecessary to mount a sustained ideological offensive to either establish or maintain their state. Given the structure of Northern politics, it is perhaps unavoidable that unionist politicians' initial reponse was to coerce the Civil Rights movement. Indeed, the priority accorded to monopolising the legal (and sometimes the illegal) means of coercion still unites most strands of unionist political opinion. Significantly, however, British intervention forestalled radical coercion policies, while replacing them with a system less responsive to the demands of popular loyalism.

The one-dimensional nature of unionist political ideology contrasted, however, with the complex differentiation of the unionist community along class and religious lines. The thrust of popular loyalism, expressed most forcefully by Paisley, was to keep that ideology simple and pure. *Within* the unionist community it had peculiarly democratic connotations – it could be formulated by any ordinary unionist as eloquently and as effectively as any political expert. As a Sandy Row shipyard worker recalled to Sarah Nelson, 'What did politics mean? Flags, parades, the red, white and blue: that's what you remember' – to which Nelson appended the comment, 'politics is a battle over things which cannot be divided, but only won or lost'.[37]

The changing material context of northern politics has also induced an awareness among unionists of the drawbacks of this one-dimensional ideology. Although this awareness takes different forms, it was powerfully reinforced by the Anglo-Irish Agreement and the resultant ideological isolation of unionists. At the level of popular unionism it was termed the last episode of a gigantic propaganda failure. Alan Wright, head of the Ulster Clubs, saw the agreement as

> the culmination of 50 years work by nationalists, not 2 years work in Dublin. Fifty years of lobbying right across the world. A 50-year PR job. We [the Loyalists] haven't being doing that and we have to learn that lesson.[38]

Also opposing the Agreement, Robert McCartney drew somewhat different conclusions. He decried the fact that it has been left to the ghettos to formulate the case for the Union:

> Those who are better equipped, by reason of their economic and intellectual status have failed to discharge their duty to the common people of Northern Ireland. That is the essential difference between the days of 1912 and the days of 1985, in 1912 we were a united people, each doing and giving according to what he had to do or give.[39]

McCartney's view is illuminating as an attempt to formulate a more liberal democratic and inclusive version of unionism opposed to the 'Protestant Sinn Feinism' of Paisley.[40] It is a lament not only for the withdrawal of intellectuals but also of northern businessmen from a politically active unionist alliance. At one remove, it could cover the so-called 'brain-drain' of unionist intellectuals and professionals from the province as a response to the troubles. More specifically, however, it highlights the dilemma of a growing number of intellectuals now instrumentally dependent on the greatly expanded state apparatus in the North (as are nationalists as well). These have to choose between a more inclusive, bureaucratic version of the British link and the appeal of popular loyalism.

John Oliver, a long-serving and senior Stormont civil servant, might stand for this group when he summed up the problem as follows:

> The unionist philosophy has become disastrously stuck in a setting appropriate no doubt to earlier times, when intransigence was the response to continuing threat, and

exclusiveness justified by smouldering rebellion. It is largely for that reason that legitimate Unionist goverments from 1921 till 1972 remained tongue-tied in so many important ways and that their extensive campaigns in Great Britain and North America were less than convincing.[41]

He goes on to make a contrast with the 'better known nationalist philosophy' sustained by 'the memory of past wrongs and nourished by the Irish or Gaelic tradition in language, literature, dancing, song, ballad, and story'. In comparison

The unionist philosophy is much less well-known and is largely misunderstood, even though it is a perfectly valid and honourable one based on the pioneering spirit, stern moral values, hard work, religious liberty, loyalty to Britain and the Crown, the maintenance of the British connection and the cherishing of British ideals.

Typically, Oliver does not elaborate the 'positive philosophy' of unionism any further. As an ideology it lacks the powerful populist appeal of Paisley's clarion call to defend Protestant Ulster.

In political terms, the debate within unionism is between 'integrationism' and Paisley-ite populism. The former is a recognition of the centrality of the British state in Northern Ireland. It reflects the curiously apolitical stance of many unionist intellectuals and middle class professionals. In oblique ways it taps a popular fatalism also that 'nothing will ever change because nothing can ever change – and what, in that situation, is the point of great initiatives and endless politics'.[42] Popular loyalism may wax and wane but it remains the standard of unionist political activism and stands for marching, Bible religion and direct action.

Conclusions

This article has attempted to show that the obstacles to political accommodation between unionists and nationalists in Ireland are at least partially rooted in the contrasting role and ideology of intellectuals on both sides. Intellectuals have not played equivalent roles on each side for deep-rooted political and structural reasons. This has inhibited the construction of a common political discourse which might inform political accommodation. It is misleading to see the conflict as a clash of abstract beliefs over religion, nationality, liberty or authority without reference to the articulators of these ideas, the way in which they have been promulgated, and the material circumstances of power and class which underpin them.

Important political and socio-economic changes have occurred which are reshaping the role and ideology of the unionist and nationalist intelligentsia. Both have become more dependent on expanded state institutions and both have grown and become differentiated. In the South the state has definitively replaced the Catholic Church as the framework of intellectual activity. The Anglo-Irish Agreement, the EC and growth of a more-specialised intelligentsia have reduced intellectual interest in the 'national question'. This has meant a distancing of the 'Northern conflict' and a re-working of a national identity more congruent with the twenty-six-county state. This has isolated the republican movement in the North.[43] Contrary to Tom Nairn's prediction, there seems to be little sign of a coherent Ulster nationalist intelligentsia emerging.

The British government's first priority is gaining acquiescence rather than popular consent for political institutions in the North – a position which may not be very different from that of the Irish government. Ideological fragmentation has proceeded apace in the North as small coteries of intellectuals adopt a variety of positions: republican, Irish nationalist, British nationalist or integrationist, socialist, liberal or Ulster nationalist. This state of flux may presage a more prominent role for intellectuals in the future. For the moment, however, their political role remains extremely limited. The mobilisation of mass consent behind agreed political structures, and the construction of a shared political vocabulary, remains as elusive as ever. Yet it remains a necessary element of any durable political settlement.

References

1. An early and prominent proponent of the 'non-bargainable' thesis was Richard Rose, *Governing without Consensus: An Irish Perspective* (London, 1971). The 'clash of identities' approach has many variants some of which see a solution in cultural pluralism. Examples of this approach may be found in Garrett Fitzgerald, *Irish Identities* (London, 1982); F.S.L. Lyons, *Culture and Anarchy in Ireland* (London, 1982); *The New Ireland Forum Report* (Dublin, 1984), and Roy Foster and the Northern Ireland Cultural Traditions Group – see Maurna Crozier, ed., *Cultural Traditions in Northern Ireland* (Belfast, 1989).

2. The range of positions reflects the depth of the political impasse. Unionists, for example, insist on the abolition or suspension of the Anglo-Irish Agreement prior to discussions; Sinn Fein seeks a British declaration to withdraw; constitutional nationalists insist on a preservation of an 'Irish dimension'. Many unionists also see the defeat of the IRA as far more important than internal political dialogue, while integrationists place the onus on the British government, or see the extension of the British party system to the North as the political priority. The failure of the political parties to bring forward an alternative to the Agreement, to advance devolution, or to develop any North-South dialogue beyond a minimal level, only serves to confirm the limits of unionist-nationalist dialogue.

3. Terence Brown, *The Whole Protestant Community: The Making of a Historical Myth* (Derry, 1985), p. 5.

4. Desmond Bell, 'Contemporary Cultural Studies in Ireland and the "Problem" of Protestant Ideology', *The Crane Bag*, Vol. 9, No. 2 (1985), 93.

5. Tom Nairn, *The Break-Up of Britain* (London, 1977), p. 241.

6. David Miller, 'One Nation vs. Two: "The Debate"', *The Irish Literary Supplement*, (Spring 1989), 47.

7. John Wilson Foster, 'Who are the Irish?', *Studies*, Vol. 77, No. 308 (1988), 412.

8. Brendan Clifford, *Queen's: Comment on a University and a Reply to its Politics Professor* (Belfast, 1988). Clifford strains credulity, however, when he asserts that public institutions under Stormont became 'in great part an apparatus of Catholic-nationalist patronage' (p. 50).

9. This distinction between intelligentsia and intellectuals follows that of G. Konrad and I. Szelenyi, *Intellectuals on the Road to Class Power* (Brighton, 1979) and Etzioni-Halevy, *The Knowledge Elite* (London, 1979). Political intellectuals are understood here as those who seek moral and intellectual leadership. In doing so, they may seek to defend or dissent from the *status quo*. Clearly, the definition of what constitutes an intellectual is contentious (see my 'Intellectuals in Twentieth-Century Ireland: The Case of George Russell (AE)', *The Crane Bag*, Vol. 9 No. 1 (1985).

10. Political intellectuals are close to the 'humanistic intellectuals' seen by Ernest Gellner in *Thought and Change* (London, 1964) to concern themselves with the records of a society, with its cultural and historical continuity and with its future. The rest of the intelligentsia are made up of scientific and technical specialists. Although the latter are less concerned with questions of teleology, neither can they completely avoid moral and political questions.

11. See Liam O'Dowd, 'Beyond Industrial Society' in P. Clancy, S. Drudy, K. Lynch and L. O'Dowd, eds., *Ireland: A Sociological Profile* (Dublin, 1986).

12. Nurses accounted for approximately 20 per cent of the professionals in each area in 1981, but the remaining professionals are in a wide variety of specialised occupations.

13. Basil Chubb, *The Government and Politics of Ireland* (London, 1982), p. 93.

14. John Harbinson, *The Ulster Unionist Party, 1882–1973* (Belfast, 1973).

15. James Dillon's labelling of De Valera as a 'pedagogue among the proletariat' could scarcely be applied to a Craig or a Brooke. See D. McCartney, *The National University of Ireland and Eamon De Valera* (Dublin, 1983).

16. Chubb, note 13, p. 92.

17. John Barkley, 'Irish Presbyterianism and the Social Order, 1920–79', unpublished paper, 1970.

18. E. B. Titley, *Church, State and the Control of Schooling, 1900–44* (Dublin, 1983).

19. John Whyte, *Church and State in Modern Ireland* (Dublin, 1971).

20. See G. L. Herries-Davies, 'Irish Thought in Science', in R. Kearney, ed., *The Irish Mind: Exploring Intellectual Traditions* (Dublin, 1985) and Roy Johnston, 'Science and Technology in Irish National Culture', *The Crane Bag*, Vol. 7, No. 2 (1983).

21. R. Cormack and R. Osborne, *Religion, Education and Employment: Aspects of Equal Opportunity in Northern Ireland* (Belfast, 1983) and R. Osborne and R. Cormack, 'Higher Education: North and South', *Administration*, Vol. 33, No. 3 (1985), 344.

22. Bell, note 4, p. 95.

23. Benedict Anderson, *Imagined Communities* (London, 1983).

24. Tom Garvin, *Nationalist Revolutionaries in Ireland* (London, 1987).

25. Gellner, note 10; Anthony Smith, *Theories of Nationalism* (New York, 1971); J. Breuilly, *Nationalism and the State* (Manchester, 1982).

26. See, for example, H. Seton Watson, *Nations and States* (London, 1977) on eastern European nationalisms.

27. See John Hutchinson, *The Dynamics of Cultural Nationalism* (London, 1987) and Roy Foster, *Modern Ireland, 1600–1972* (Harmondsworth, 1988).

28. This intellectual 'community' still provides a compelling reference-point for Irish intellectuals today, especially those who address the relationship between literature, art, philosophy and contemporary Irish politics. Examples can be seen in journals such as *The Crane Bag*, *The Irish Review*, and the Field Day publications.

29. Personal interview with Estyn Evans. One of the more typical complaints of contemporary Protestant intellectuals in the North is that they were denied a knowledge, not only of Irish, but also of Ulster literature and culture while at school. It is perhaps significant that it was Evans, a Welshman, who was mainly responsible for pioneering Ulster and Irish cultural studies within Queen's University between 1930 and 1970.

30. See Rex Cathcart, *The Most Contrary Region: The BBC in Northern Ireland, 1924–1984* (Belfast, 1984).

31. Examples include Geoff Bell, *The Protestants of Ulster* (London, 1976); David Miller, *Queen's Rebels: Ulster Loyalism in Historical Perspective* (Dublin, 1978); Ron Wiener, *The Rape and Plunder of the Shankill* (Belfast, 1980); Richard Jenkins, *Lads, Citizens and Ordinary Kids* (London, 1983); Sarah Nelson, *Ulster's Uncertain Defenders* (Belfast, 1984); Roy Wallis, Steve Bruce and David Taylor, *"No Surrender": Paisleyism and the Politics of Ethnic Identity in Northern Ireland* (Belfast, 1986); Steve Bruce, *God Save Ulster! The Religion and Politics of Paisleyism* (Oxford, 1987); Desmond Bell, 'Acts of Union: Youth Culture and Ethnic Identity amongst Protestants in Northern Ireland', *British Journal of Sociology*, Vol. 38, No. 2, 158–183. Besides Bruce's work there are now no less than four biographies of Paisley – Patrick Marrinan, *Paisley: Man of Wrath* (Tralee, 1973); Ed Moloney and Andy Pollak, *Paisley* (Dublin, 1986); Clifford Smyth, *Ian Paisley: The Voice of Protestant Ulster* (Edinburgh, 1987), and Rhonda Paisley, *Ian Paisley: My Father* (Basingstoke, 1988).

32. Nelson, note 31, p. 9.

33. Desmond Bell, note 4, p. 93.

34. The United Irishmen, the fate of nineteenth-century Liberal Unionism, the Labour and socialist movements in Ulster, and more recently, O'Neillism, are examples of failed attempts to make lasting links between loyalism and nationalism, liberal democracy, and socialism.

35. Desmond Bell, note 4, p. 95.

36. See Oliver MacDonagh's brilliant discussion of 'politics clerical' in *States of Mind* (London, 1985).

37. Nelson, note 31, p. 37.

38. Interview in *Fortnight*, 10–23 February, 1986.

39. *NI Assembly Debates*, Vol. 18, No. 4, 16 November 1985 on the Anglo-Irish Agreement.

40. See Robert MacCartney, *Liberty and Authority in Ireland* (Derry, 1985).

41. John Oliver, *Ulster Today and Tomorrow* (London, 1978), p. 68.

42. See Michael Diskin's comment on Official Unionism in the *Irish Times*, 26 November 1986.

43. One acerbic observer has noted: 'In the 1970s the Southern middle class conceded traditional nationalism to the Northern working class. Since then their intellectuals have been trying to fashion an ideology which can integrate their material interests with a sense of national purpose. Many have found a substitute in an obsession with the budget deficit, but that hardly constitutes an ideology. . . .' Gene Kerrigan, 'Television and Radio' (review) *Sunday Tribune*, 12 March 1989. Ulick O'Connor also criticises the refusal of Irish writers to adopt a national stance on the Northern conflict. See *Crisis and Commitment: The Writer and Northern Ireland* (Dublin, 1989).

Index